ANCI
HEAL
TECHNIQUES

To Write to the Author

If you wish to contact the author or would like more information about this book, please write to the author in care of Llewellyn Worldwide and we will forward your request. Both the author and publisher appreciate hearing from you and learning of your enjoyment of this book and how it has helped you. Llewellyn Worldwide cannot guarantee that every letter written to the author can be answered, but all will be forwarded. Please write to:

Douglas De Long
℅ Llewellyn Worldwide
P.O. Box 64383, Dept. 0-7387-0650-7
St. Paul, MN 55164-0383, U.S.A.

Please enclose a self-addressed stamped envelope for reply,
or $1.00 to cover costs. If outside U.S.A., enclose
international postal reply coupon.

Many of Llewellyn's authors have websites with additional information and resources. For more information, please visit our website at http://www.llewellyn.com.

ANCIENT HEALING TECHNIQUES

A
Course in
Psychic
& Spiritual
Development

Douglas De Long

Llewellyn Publications
St. Paul, Minnesota

First Edition
First Printing, 2005

Book design by Donna Burch
Cover design by Ellen Dahl
Cover photo ©2005 by Digital Stock
Interior art by Ellen Dahl

Llewellyn is a registered trademark of Llewellyn Worldwide, Ltd.

Library of Congress Cataloging-in-Publication Data
ISBN: 0-7387-0650-7
(Pending)

Llewellyn Publications
A Division of Llewellyn Worldwide, Ltd.
P.O. Box 64383, Dept. 0-7387-0650-7
St. Paul, MN 55164-0383, U.S.A.
www.llewellyn.com

Printed in the United States of America

Also by Douglas De Long

Ancient Teachings for Beginners

Contents

Charts and Illustrations

Chapter 4

Chapter 5

Chapter 6

Chapter 7

Chapter 8

Chapter 9

Techniques and Exercises

Preface

Ancient Healing Techniques is an advanced course in psychic and spiritual development, and ancient techniques for healing. It is designed for those of you who are spiritually and psychically awakened or "initiated." It is a continuation of my first book, *Ancient Teachings for Beginners.*

> "The advancement of our minds and souls
> is the ultimate achievement."
>
> —Douglas De Long

Introduction

A Message

"Light shines out and joy pours forth . . ."
—The Dead Sea Scrolls, column 27, 4Q, 427,
fragment 7, page 113.

The world is changing in a special way. Humanity is raising its consciousness to a greater height. This means that many people's personal vibrations have increased to a new spiritual level. Simply put, you are now using more parts of your brain that are linked to psychic and spiritual attributes. This is the start of true enlightenment. In the near future, earthly science will understand all this.

Along with the raising of human consciousness, the energy or vibration of the planet has risen dramatically. This has allowed our earthly realm to develop a nearness to heaven, or more accurately, the heavenly fields. It is much closer to Earth than you realize. In the past, there was a great distance between these two realms. This made it more difficult for people to commune with angels, spirit guides, and other light beings associated with the heavenly realm.

These two events, the raising of the Earth's vibrations and the raising of human consciousness, are creating wonderful possibilities for many people. This indicates that it is far easier to meet and work with angels and spirit guides. There is more opportunity than ever before to communicate with heavenly messengers, spiritual teachers, angelic healers, and other representatives of the hierarchy of the heavenly fields. This is not your imagination. Please pay attention to what you hear inside and what you feel in your heart.

As you become more spiritually and psychically advanced in life, you will begin to realize certain truths pertaining to heaven and earth. Everyone has his or her own spiritual path to follow. Religion is one of these paths that can lead many people back to the Creator or Godsource. However, a religion or spiritual belief based on a male-dominated or patriarchal system is incomplete and unbalanced. Humanity is represented by both sexes. Life is created and thrives on the male and female energies. The very survival of our species depends on these two aspects working together in harmony. A religion should fully reflect this concept in its doctrine.

In the heavenly fields, the male and female can be found in God or the Creator. Our Supreme Being is both the Father and the Mother. Our Father in heaven would be better described as Our Father and Mother in heaven. The divine essence of the heavenly fields needs both these energies to exist and flourish. Why would the earthly realm be any different? As the old adage says, "as above, so below."

This same principle is true in regards to ancient healing techniques. Both male and female energies, sometimes referred to as Yin and Yang, are important for true healing to manifest. The Master Jesus taught this concept to the many men and women who became his students and disciples. This included members of his family. His decision to teach his knowledge and hidden secrets to both sexes two thousand years ago went against the traditions of that time and place. This was accomplished through his own secret society.

In his book *The Secret Doctrines of Jesus*, H. Spencer Lewis, late imperator of the Rosicrucians, refers to this:

> That among the one hundred and twenty members were not those who were later known as the Twelve Disciples and who constituted the secret executive committee of this secret society, but also others who were interested in the mysterious, secret work of the society, including the mother of Jesus and his brothers and sisters.

Unfortunately, biblical history tends to ignore this fact. The written records called the Gospels of the New Testament mention several women as being associated with Jesus. Along with Mother Mary, there was Mary Magdalene. She worked as an energy healer and herbalist. She was not a prostitute as the Gospels wrongly portrayed her. She was closely associated with Jesus, who trained her in the ancient mysteries. Mary Magdalene used her secret knowledge and gifts and became a wonderful healer.[1] The close connection between her and the Master Jesus is also referred to in my previous book, *Ancient Teachings for Beginners,* in the last chapter.

There is another matter that should be discussed at this time. A power struggle between the forces of good and evil is culminating in the not-too-distant future. Many of you will see this event in your lifetimes.

The spiritual teacher Zoroaster spoke of the battle between the Sons of Light and the Sons of Darkness, almost five hundred years before Christ. The ancient Persians, who followed the teachings of this Master Teacher, believed in a god of light and goodness. This deity was known as "Mithra."

The Magi, associated with the ancient Persians, were a group of wise philosophers and astronomers. They fully embraced these same ancient teachings and beliefs. The story of the three wise men or Magi mentioned in the New Testament is probably based on these well-known scholars.

As another Master Teacher, Jesus made allusions to the same struggle during his ministry. Similar statements can be found in certain texts of the Dead Sea Scrolls, as per example.

> "The first attack of the Sons of Light shall be undertaken against the forces of the Sons of Darkness, the army of Belial . . ."
>
> —The War Scroll,
> Column 1, 1QM, 4Q, 491–496.
> The Dead Sea Scrolls, p. 151.

There are many doomsayers who use the book of Revelations in the Bible to proclaim a terrible future for us all. Several religious groups believe an end is near. These proclamations of gloom and doom need not be so. As more people become initiated or enlightened, they attune themselves to the Creator or Godsource. A wonderful transformation, not an end, will be the ultimate outcome.

As stated, humanity has raised its consciousness. A major spiritual awakening has arisen. A search for spiritual truth stirs your souls. As this occurs, more of you will refrain from actions that are of a negative and unbeneficial nature. You will change and develop more loving ways.

"In doubt if an action is just, abstain."
—Zoroaster (c. 630–553 BCE)

Truth, hidden knowledge, and ancient secrets kept from the masses in the past are now being revealed to humanity as it becomes more enlightened. As you awaken and start to use more of your mind power and psychic abilities, the secrets and hidden mysteries will be unveiled to you.

In the following pages of ancient teaching, unique lessons that originated in ancient times from mystery schools and healing temples will be covered in detail. These wonderful places of learning existed in the lands of Egypt, Persia, and other areas. Jesus was one of many whom embraced these teachings. These lessons or teachings are specifically designed to help you become professional energy healers, medical intuitives, spiritual counselors, and teachers. You may find yourselves embracing all or some of these careers in your own work in the near future. For those of you already involved in these fast-growing fields, the techniques in this book will allow you to enhance your own gifts. The ancient ways of healing, teaching and counseling are fast becoming modern ways of life for millions worldwide.

As you use more of your psychic and spiritual abilities, you will work with your spirit helpers and angels. Also, you will help to raise the vibrations or consciousness of many individuals. This will result in a larger portion of humanity being "enlightened," and thus the Sons and Daughters of Light will triumph over darkness and evil.

After reflecting upon the message just given you, the following short account will help to put everything into perspective. Let your mind open up and enjoy the event.

It is three thousand years ago in the land of ancient Egypt. Imagine yourself there as an initiated student belonging to one of the mystery schools and healing temples. For many years you have studied the ancient mysteries along with special healing techniques.

You can remember that night several years ago, the night you stood before the Great Sphinx. It was here at this sacred place that you and many others were initiated into the mystery school through a ritual called the First Initiation. A priest dressed in a white robe and standing next to the burning altar looked upon each and every one of you. That was the beginning of your studies in the ancient mysteries. It was also the beginning of your lifelong spiritual journey.

Now years later you have achieved your goals, you have become more spiritually awakened. Many of your psychic abilities have opened up like a flower to the sun. You have become one of the "Initiated." You are ready for your advanced training at this mystery school and healing temple. The living waters of the Nile flow by the complex as you lean against a large column, allowing your mind to dream.

> "Heaven is my father, the earth my mother, and even a tiny creature such as myself finds an intimate place in their midst. In everything that moves through the universe, I see my own body, and in everything that governs the universe, my own soul. All are my brethren, and all things my companions."
>
> —Chang Tsai (1021–1077), Chinese philosopher

Endnote

1. There is more archaeological and historical evidence suggesting that Mary Magdalene was a healer and came from the small fishing village of Magda, not far from Caperneum. She may also have been known as Miriam. The Gnostic Gospels contain some material about her.

Chapter 1

The Final Initiation: Part One

> "If there is anything lovely, if there is anything
> desirable, if there is anything within the reach
> of man that is worthy of praise, is it not knowl-
> edge?"
>
> —Sri Ramatherin

In the ancient mystery schools and healing temples that existed throughout Egypt thousands of years ago, advanced
initiates or students took part in a special rite or initiation.
This was called the "Final Initiation" and was performed by
the High Priest of each respective school. For the fortunate
students, this secret ceremony was conducted inside the
Great Pyramid, within what is now known as the King's
Chamber. All other initiates not able to attend the rite at
this ancient structure received their Final Initiation at various places throughout Egypt, such as the Sacred Lake at
Karnak.

In any case, the Final Initiation was performed in exactly the same manner by all of the ancient mystery schools and healing temples. For all participants, the event took place within the Great Pyramid in either an actual or symbolic way. The results of this secret initiation had a profound effect on the advanced students.

It should also be known that this wonderful ceremony originated in the healing and teaching temples and pyramids of Atlantis. When some of these advanced people migrated to Egypt over ten thousand years ago, they brought this and other knowledge with them, resulting in a pre-Egyptian civilization consisting of strong spiritual beliefs.

The Final Initiation took place at midnight and was performed by the High Priest and advanced students together. All of them gathered in the central reception chamber beneath the Great Sphinx (see figure 1.1, page 12). The High Priest of the Egyptian mystery school then led them through a long hallway and into a slightly smaller chamber. Three hallways led from this chamber. One hallway went directly north under the Great Pyramid. A secret stairway connected the hallway to the interior of this ancient building. All of the advanced students were guided by the High Priest through the hallway, up the stone stairs, and into the lower part of the Great Pyramid. (Today, there is only a large gaping hole remaining at this place.) From here, they walked up one long passageway and then turned left and climbed up another long passageway. This passageway is now known as the Grand Gallery. Together they approached a low door opening, bent down, and entered an upper chamber that was deep inside this ancient structure.

Sandalwood incense burned within this chamber, the King's Chamber. The few special initiates gathered in a small circle around their spiritual teacher, the High Priest of the ancient mystery school and healing temple. A single torch also burned within this inner sanctum.

A deep breathing exercise prepared everyone for the initiation, which the High Priest guided the participants through. Once the exercise was completed, all the students allowed themselves to enter into a relaxed, meditative state of consciousness. It was at this point that the spiritual teacher commenced with the ritual. This involved the chanting or toning of a special, powerful word. The initiates started to chant as well. They all continued chanting in a methodical manner.

The Final Initiation lasted for about ten minutes. When completed, everyone, including the High Priest, had been intensely affected by the vibrations created by this word chant. The advanced students, the initiated, originally consisting of both men and women, were now ready to begin their work in the outside world.

In this chapter you will learn the Final Initiation techniques used by the ancients in their mystery schools and healing temples. As advanced students, you will benefit greatly by performing the breathing and chanting exercises. An enhancement of some of your psychic and spiritual abilities will be the desired result. It is specifically designed for you, the initiated and advanced student.

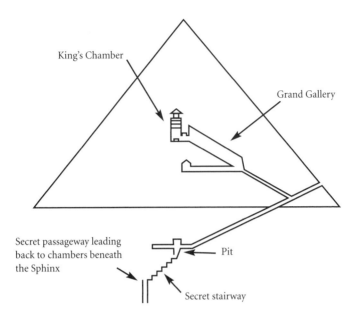

Figure 1.1: Interior of Great Pyramid, including secret stairs and passageway.

This means that you have been on the spiritual and psychic path for many years or have in a shorter time developed several of your own gifts. You understand and are knowledgeable about human auras, chakras, channeling, reincarnation, energy healing, clairvoyance, and other psychic phenomena. Many of you may already be working in complementary and alternative healing modalities. There will be some of you who work in the normal, mundane world but use your abilities to create a better life for yourselves and loved ones.

Before performing the special chant, you must begin with a certain breathing exercise. This exercise must be done first for specific reasons. By taking breath into the lungs, you draw in the universal energy that is also referred to as chi or spirit energy. This is the energy, the essence of the Creator, that exists everywhere. It is in the air, in the trees, the rocks, the earth, and the water.

In the culture of the Cree Indians of North America, rocks are considered living entities. This makes perfect sense if you regard our Mother Earth as a living being that supports all forms of life, including rocks.

When you breathe the Universal Energy into your body, you start to alter your brainwave patterns. This relaxes you and thus allows you to enter more easily into altered states of consciousness. The chi or Universal Energy also changes the vibrational level of your being and even affects the electromagnetism within. This phenomenon will be covered in detail much later in another chapter.

Heart Chakra Breathing Technique

Begin by taking a deep breath into your lungs through your nose. Feel your chest expanding as you draw in the air that contains the chi or Universal Energy. This allows the heart chakra or center to open up slightly. After inhaling, hold your breath for about five seconds. The Universal Energy that is contained within your lungs will start to affect your whole body by recharging your circulatory system with this energy. This spirit or chi energy will then work its way through your whole being. Your aura or human energy field will start to expand. You will start to become more re-laxed and centered.

After five seconds have elapsed, release your breath slowly and evenly through your mouth. Wait a moment and then repeat this process two more times. Doing this breathing exercise a total of three times has the greatest ef-fect on your body and your aura.

Now just relax for a few moments, letting your mind wander.

Solar Plexus Chakra Breathing Technique

When you are ready, take in another deep breath through your nose, this time drawing the breath deep down inside into your diaphragm. By concentrating on your solar plexus as you breathe in, you will feel this area rising if you are doing the technique correctly. Hold the breath for about five seconds. This will draw the chi or Universal Energy into the solar plexus thereby activating this center slightly.

As in the Heart Chakra Breathing Technique, evenly re-lease your breath through your open mouth. Repeat the Solar Plexus Breathing Technique twice more and then let yourself relax. Allow your mind to drift.

The Final Initiation

You are now ready to do the Final Initiation as the ad-vanced initiates did long ago inside the Great Pyramid. Both the heart and solar plexus chakras have been properly activated a bit. Your brain wave patterns have slowed down and thus your mind is in a receptive state.

This ancient initiation involves the use of a sound created by the letters A, M, and E. These three letters are placed together as AME. This AME rhymes with "game" and is chanted in a specific manner.

When chanted in the proper sequence, all seven major chakras will be affected. AME should be chanted a total of nine times. This chanting or toning should be divided into three sets.

The first set consisting of three chants of AME will be attempted in such a way as to affect the pineal and pituitary glands, and the hypothalamus region of the brain. This in turn will affect the crown chakra, located on the top of the head, and the third eye chakra in the forehead. These two chakras will be activated and opened. The throat chakra will also be slightly affected.

This special sound will be expressed in a mid-to-high C musical note. If you are not well versed in music, do not worry; an approximation of the desired frequency is fine. The sound you are striving for is not too high and not too low, but simply at a midrange between a high tenor note and a deep bass note.

Begin the first set of the exercise by taking in a deep breath through your nose. Hold it for a few moments and then chant A-A-A-M-M-M-E as you slowly and evenly expel all your breath. Remember that it sounds like "game" without the "g." Try to feel a resonance or vibration within your head as you attempt this. After your breath has been released, let yourself relax for a few seconds.

Then repeat the process. This time focus on your third eye chakra as you intone AME. Let the vibration work into this area. You may feel a slight pressure or sensation in the middle of your forehead or even an inch within. As an advanced or initiated person, you are sensitive to energy and will probably feel some sensation in this area very easily. After you have released your breath, relax again for a few seconds. Allow the pressure or sensation to continue on its own without you trying to concentrate on it any more. If you do not feel any sensation, do not worry, the process is still working.

When ready, repeat the process a third and final time. In this case, as you chant A-A-M-M-E, focus your attention on the top of the head in the crown chakra region. Feel yourself directing the vibrational sound up through the brain and into this area. You may start to experience tingling sensations or pressure here during or immediately following the chant. This is normal and is the desired effect. Once you have exhaled all your breath, allow yourself to relax. Go back to normal breathing. Just let your mind drift for a few moments.

After this short interval, you are now ready to start the second set of chants or tones. Certain physiological effects are taking place within your brain and body by now.

The second set of chants will be expressed in a slightly lower musical note or sound. The proper frequency to use should be a mid-C note. By lowering your voice to just below the level used previously, you will affect the throat and heart chakras.

Begin again by taking a deep breath into your lungs. Hold it for three or four seconds. Then, as in the first set of chants, release your breath slowly through your mouth intoning A-A-A-M-M-M-E. Feel the vibration or frequency in your throat and chest as you expel all your breath. Make sure that you focus on these two chakras while chanting AME. You may wish to raise or lower your voice slightly as you experiment with this sound. Everyone is unique and different. Therefore a note or two below mid-C may be more effective for some of you. For others the mid-C note may have the best effect.

When you have done this chant once at the desired frequency, wait a few seconds. Then repeat the process and try to feel yourself directing this vibration or sound into the throat and heart. Feel the chant going deep inside these two areas of the body. You may experience a slight pressure or sensation in one or both of these chakras as you chant AME. In some cases you might feel a vibration, pulsing, or pleasing sensation in these chakras after completing the chant.

Go back to normal breathing for a few seconds. Once more, take in another deep breath and repeat the process. This time, concentrate fully on your chest and heart chakras. Allow the vibrational sound of AME to resonate within your chest. Enjoy the effects of this chant inside you. When you have released all your breath, return to normal breathing. Let yourself stare off into space and allow your thoughts to wander for a brief period.

This second set of chants performed in an approximate mid-C note will create a vibration or resonance within these two areas. This in turn helps to open up the throat and heart chakras. On a physical level, other effects are occurring.

After completing the first two sets of chants, you may start to feel spacey or light-headed. This is normal. Tingling sensations or slight pressures may be experienced by many of you. This is an indication that the vibrational chants are starting to work properly.

The third set of chants should be completed in a slightly different manner from the first two sets. This time draw a deep breath down into your diaphragm. The Solar Plexus Breathing Technique that you just read about should be employed. After holding your breath for no more than five seconds, release it slowly and evenly through your mouth as you tone A-A-A-M-M-M-E in a deeper voice than you used last time. The ideal note should be a low C or just slightly above it. For most women, chanting this sound in a deep voice should suffice. For many men, lowering your voice to a bass level and then bringing the sound up a bit will create the approximate sound needed. As stated before, everyone is different and can be more attuned to certain sounds. Find the exact vibrational sound that works best for you by raising or lowering your voice slightly as you chant A-A-A-M-M-M-E.

While toning this sound as you expel all your breath, focus your attention on the solar plexus just above the navel area of your body. Feel a warmth or tingling sensation, or even a slight vibration here. Try to direct the sound into this chakra as you concentrate.

Once more, relax for a few seconds. Return to normal breathing. Some of you may feel certain sensations in the solar plexus chakra. Chakras are not stationary but move and shift gently, similar to the way the Northern Lights dance in a winter evening sky. The solar plexus chakra as a general rule is usually one to three inches above the belly button. The sacral chakra is about the same distance below the navel.

After a very brief respite, repeat the process. This time focus your attention below your navel in the sacral chakra region. Try to direct the AME tone here. Imagine or feel a vibration within. After your breath has been released, relax again and return to normal breathing.

When ready, repeat the process a third and final time. In this case, concentrate all your attention into the reproductive organs where the base chakra is located. Direct the vibrational sound here as you chant. Feel the resonation or vibration within the base. You might even experience some warmth or a pleasant sensation in this area.

Once you have completed the third set of chants, let your mind wander as your breathing becomes regular again. If you are successful, there should be several things happening now that you may or may not be aware of. Both the psychic and physiological effects created by performing the Final Initiation will be explained later.

Psychic Effects

· Clairvoyant abilities (to see beyond the norm) enhanced

· Clairaudient abilities (to hear beyond the norm) enhanced

· Clairsentient abilities (to feel or sense beyond the norm) enhanced

· Creativity enhanced

· Intuitive abilities enhanced

· Empathic abilities enhanced

· Healing abilities increased

· Attunement to the Creator or Godsource

· Awareness of past lives and knowledge from those periods

· Soul travel abilities developed or enhanced

· Higher vibrations of energy received in aura and chakras

· Your higher purpose understood

Some or many of the psychic abilities just mentioned will be fine-tuned. This means that certain gifts or abilities will work at their most efficient level. You will become more psychic and spiritual in nature. This allows you to take control of your own life and master your own future.

Chapter 2

The Final Initiation: Part Two

"The key to happiness and wisdom lies within
you."

—Douglas De Long

Physiological Effects

As stated in my previous book *Ancient Teachings for Beginners,* the proper sound expressed by chanting or toning at a certain frequency or musical note creates a vibration inside the head that causes the pineal glands to vibrate or resonate. The energy manifested by the vibrating or resonating gland will work into the hypothalamus, where the body's pleasure center is located. Also, the chanting exercises of the Final Initiation affect other parts of the body, including organs and glands. The endocrine glandular system that is connected to the seven major chakras is influenced greatly by performing the Final Initiation.

The toning of the powerful sound of AME causes the major chakras consisting of the crown, third eye, throat, heart, solar plexus, sacral plexus, and base chakras to vibrate. This vibration along with the sound itself sends a resonation or energy into the sympathetic nervous system. The sympathetic and parasympathetic nervous divisions of the autonomic nervous system run along both sides of the spine's central nervous system. This vibration affects the SND, and in turn transmits a high vibration of energy through the nerve plexus into the central nervous system. From here, this energy, along with natural nerve energy, branches out of the nervous system into the body's glands and organs. A large percentage of these energies go directly into the glands associated with the endocrine system. These glands are the pineal, the thyroid, the thymus gland, the pituitary, the adrenals, the pancreas, and the gonads (ovaries or testes).

The AME chant will also directly affect these glands causing them to vibrate or resonate within the body. This allows certain physiological events to happen. As the glands of the endocrine system receive the energies via the SND and central nervous system, healing light created by both the nerve energy and vibrational energy permeates these glands. They all start to function at a higher frequency.

Rates of Vibration

All organs, glands, and cells of the human body work at different frequencies or rates of vibration. In physics, rates of vibration are expressed as cycles per second (cps) or hertz (Hz). One hertz equals one cycle per second. This measurement is used for all vibrations. Everything upon the earth vibrates or resonates. A rock has a different rate of vibration than a tree, and a tree has a different vibration or frequency than a bird. This holds true with the human body. Each gland, organ, and cell of the human body functions properly at specific frequencies or vibratory rates. They all have slightly different frequencies or cycles per second than each other, but work together in harmony; they are synchronized. The human body, itself, has a designated vibratory rate that sets the mark for the glands, organs, and cells contained inside it.

If you can think of a beautiful symphony playing in harmony, then you can understand the principle behind all of this. When a gland, organ, or cell starts to lose its frequency, it becomes "out of sync" with the surrounding glands and cells. This means that it is off frequency and creates a disharmony. If this improper rate of vibration continues for a long period of time, a serious health problem arises. The gland, organ, or cell that is out of frequency with the surrounding parts will become diseased. In some cases it will become cancerous. Once again, it is the same idea as one violin player in the symphony playing out of tune with the rest.

By toning or chanting special sounds in a specified musical note, a vibration can work into the glands, organs, and cells, as well as the chakras and aura. This helps to regulate the vibrational rates of the respective organ or body part. In other words, chanting assists in putting an off-frequency gland, organ, or cell back into its proper frequency and it also keeps the other ones in frequency and in attunement. In certain circumstances, early stages of cancer can be reversed with the use of special chants. This is sometimes referred to as "sound therapy."

In the near future, medical science will recognize the tremendous value of "energy" or "vibrational work." Lights, sounds, colors, and music will all be used together to heal and even prevent diseases during the twenty-first century. At this time, there is no technologically advanced equipment available to measure the true vibratory rates of the organs, glands, and cells of the human body.

When you do your own work on your chakras or energy centers and practice toning as well, a high vibration of energy enters into your auric field, chakras, and physical body. This allows the physical form to raise its vibrations, meaning that the vibratory rate associated with your body starts to increase to a higher frequency.

The following comparison may help. Think of your body as an AM radio station. Through certain procedures you can change or raise the frequency of the station until it becomes an FM radio station. Most of you are aware that FM, or frequency-modulated waves, are much higher and give better sound quality than AM, or amplitude-modulated radio waves.

When you raise your own frequency or vibratory rate, light from the Godsource or the Creator enters into your being. This light is the divine energy or universal energy that descends from the heavenly fields and manifests upon the earth. A part of this high energy is the Holy Spirit or Holy Ghost often mentioned in the Bible.

In essence, more light from God can pour forth into your body and affect the glands, organs, and cells. These all begin to vibrate at slightly higher frequencies and possess more light within. Thus you become a light being within the physical, leading to a closer connection to the Creator and the heavenly fields. Keep in mind that the Godsource is composed of both male and female energies.

The higher your body's vibratory rate, the better chance of maintaining a healthy and disease-free body. This is one of the many reasons why the Final Initiation is very important.

Chakras, Endocrine Glands, and Hormones

The toning or chanting techniques of the Final Initiation have a profound effect upon the chakras and endocrine glandular system.

The first set of chants causes the pineal gland to vibrate or resonate, and release the hormone melatonin into the bloodstream, helping to make you feel better emotionally. The pineal gland is partially responsible for creating a feeling of well-being inside of you. The vibrating pineal also influences the hypothalamus where, as stated before, the pleasure center is located. Natural endorphins will then be released into the bloodstream, and help to achieve a natural high, a sense of elation.

The pituitary gland will also be greatly affected by the first set of chants. This gland consists of two portions, the front portion called the anterior pituitary and the back portion called the posterior pituitary. Both portions complement each other but have distinct functions. It is the anterior pituitary that exerts direct influence on many of the other glands of the endocrine system.

It should be mentioned at this time that there is a Divine Intelligence involved in all of this. The brain itself performs its many functions in a purely electromechanical manner. It is the mind, a part of the human soul, that directs everything and works in conjunction with the chanting process and the desired results. Your mind works as a safeguard and helps to regulate the physical brain and endocrine system. Keep this thought clearly in mind as you continue to read.

When you chant AME three times in a high-to-mid-C musical note, both portions of the pituitary gland will vibrate immediately or shortly afterward. When this happens, the front portion will release the following hormonal secretions: human growth hormone (HGH), thyrotropic hormone, prolactin, and melanophore stimulating hormone (MSH). Human growth hormone is the most abundant hormone in the anterior pituitary. HGH stimulates body growth and regulates metabolism. The thyrotropic secretion will stimulate the thyroid and assists in balancing this gland in the throat. MSH affects the skin's pigmentation, helping to create healthy-looking skin. Prolactin is used for milk production in nursing women and for assisting in penile erection in males. The benefits are obvious. This secretion also affects and regulates menstrual cycles in females. For many women, this may or may not be considered a benefit!

Human Growth Hormone

There is something special that should be noted about human growth hormone. This secretion lessens in adulthood and between the ages of thirty-five and forty, HGH is secreted even less. This results in the start of the aging process! Therefore by doing this chant you will slow down or even reverse your own aging. There will be a significant increase of the human growth hormone into the system. This balances the body metabolism. For those of you over thirty-five, the potential benefits are even greater. Your skin may start to look younger and your eyes will become brighter and clearer.

The back or posterior pituitary does not produce its own secretions, but instead stores and releases hormones that are produced within the hypothalamus. This part of the brain extends and attaches itself to the posterior pituitary. Once again, it is the human mind as part of the immortal soul that regulates and decides which secretions to release into the bloodstream and what chemical signals to send to other glands of the endocrine system. Your mind, which is connected to the Godsource above, also knows how much of a certain secretion to release and when. Chapter 3 will go into greater detail about the mind and brain.

This first set of chants also creates a vibration through all of the brain, not just the pituitary, pineal, and hypothalamus. This vibration sends energy into the hypothalamus and then upwards into the thalamus area. The thalamus is above the midbrain region and is oval-shaped. At the same time, energy vibrates down into the brain stem. The hypothalamus is located in the lower part of the brain in close proximity to the pineal and pituitary glands (see figure 2.1).

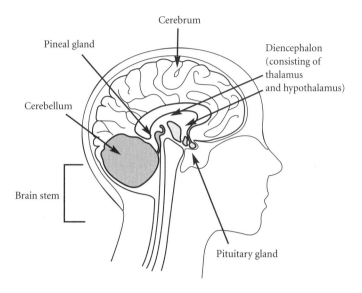

Figure 2.1: Location of pineal, pituitary, thalamus, and hypothalamus. Note their proximity to one another.

When the vibration created by chanting AME in a high-to-mid-C musical note works into these areas of the brain, the hypothalamus, thalamus, and brain stem, a special physiological event takes place. An hormonal secretion called serotonin is released by these stimulated and energized areas.

Serotonin is directly involved in mood control, sleep regulation, sensory perception, and learning. When proper amounts of this hormone are released, a person feels more balanced, sleeps better, feels more alive, and retains information more easily. Moods swings are very minor and sensory perception is normal. An individual will even have a healthy appetite.

When serotonin levels become low within the brain, serious results can occur. Medical science refers to people who are depressed or "bipolar" as having a chemical imbalance within the brain. This imbalance, of course, refers to serotonin. Aggressiveness, suicidal tendencies, depression, sleeplessness, and major mood swings are some of the effects of this hormonal imbalance. Many people take drugs such as Paxil and Prozac to counteract the effects of low serotonin levels.

If you learn to work with your own chakras and do toning or chanting, you can balance the endocrine glandular system including the pineal and pituitary glands and other areas in the brain. For someone suffering from low serotonin levels, a steady, positive effect may result. Within a few weeks or even a few days, the serotonin levels will increase and eventually reach a healthy, balanced level. As this happens, individuals on mood-control drugs may slowly start to wean themselves off the medication. The decision to do so should be an individual's choice. Everyone is different and therefore each person is affected differently by chanting and performing chakra energy work. Some of you who suffer with this malady may feel instant results while many of you may notice slight, subtle changes. For a few, little or no results may occur. In this case, a very real physiological problem may exist within the brain and thus only conservative medical treatments with drugs will work.

Fortunately not everyone who suffers from low serotonin levels needs to rely on the standard medical approach.

Many people who have practiced meditation, chanting, and energy work have succeeded in freeing themselves from this affliction. It is also recommended to check with your physician and follow this method in a slow, careful manner.

Once you have balanced your glandular system, you will continue to feel happier, more relaxed, and appreciative of life. Mood swings become less and you start to develop a sense of peace or "at oneness." This holds true for everyone, not just people affected by low serotonin levels or chemical imbalances.

The first set of chants of the Final Initiation profoundly affect the crown and third eye chakras, opening them up like a flower reacting to the sunshine. When these energy centers are opened, they become activated or energized. This allows the Universal Energy, natural chi, or healing energy to descend from the heavenly fields above and enter through your crown chakra at the top of your head. This energy is also referred to in the Bible as the Holy Spirit or Holy Ghost. This same powerful energy can be found everywhere on the earth and surrounds all of us.

The throat chakra is affected slightly by this chant, too. As mentioned earlier, the thyroid and parathyroids that are associated with this energy center are affected and have an influence upon the rest of the endocrine system (see figure 2.2 on pages 32 and 33).

For the majority of people, the second set of chants of the Final Initiation will greatly influence the throat and heart chakras. This chanting also affects the thyroid and parathyroids and thymus gland. As a result, these areas are stimulated and start to function in a more harmonious manner.

If the thyroid gland is underactive, this chant will help to speed it up. Eventually the thyroid will become more balanced and function in a healthy and proper manner if you practice this and other techniques.

Always bear in mind that each individual is different and unique. Everyone experiences things in his or her own way. For many people, all three sets of chants will influence them greatly. For some, the effects will be more subtle. There are a few persons who may not feel or experience a beneficial change by performing the second set of chants initially. In some situations, chakra energy-flow techniques that were discussed in *Ancient Teachings for Beginners,* and some advanced techniques covered later in chapters 6 and 7, may be more productive for you. Nevertheless, the second set of chants will still affect you internally, whether you are aware of it or not. Divine Intelligence prevails.

The thyroid gland will release thyroid hormones that regulate the biochemical reactions within the body. This is commonly referred to as the rate of metabolism. This is important because it keeps the endocrine system in harmony and helps to slow down the aging process. Oxygen consumption is increased within the body, which results in more Universal Energy, chi or vital life force being available within, also.

The central nervous system, especially the nerve tissues, can be affected in a positive manner by the thyroid. These tissues become healthier, allowing more nerve energy to flow through the nerves and into organs and glands.

The body temperature is better regulated after completing the second set of chants. For those of you who feel cold most of the time, this may help to warm you up.

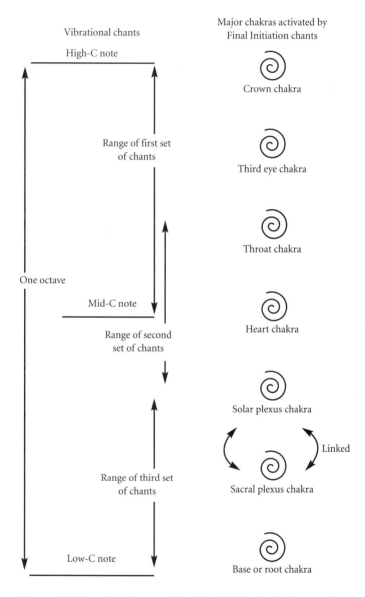

Figure 2.2: How the chants of the Final Initiation influence the major chakras, endocrine glands, and hormonal secretions

Endocrine glands influenced and stimulated by activated chakras	Some hormonal secretions resulting from activated chakras and stimulated endocrine glands
Pituitary (Hypothalamus)	Human Growth Hormone (HGH), thyrotropic hormone, prolactin, Melanophore Stimulating Hormone (MSH)
Pineal	Serotonin Melatonin
Thyroid and Parathyroid	Thyroid hormones Parathyroid Hormone (PTH)
Thymus	T cells (T3, T4)
Adrenals	Steroids, Sexual hormones
Pancreas	Glucagon, insulin, digestive enzymes
Reproductive organs (Sacral plexus chakra) (Base or root chakra)	Testosterone (male) Estrogens, Progesterone (female)

The secretion of thyroid hormones along with HGH or the human growth hormone accelerates body growth in children and teenagers.

The second set of chants of the Final Initiation will activate the throat chakra, influence and stimulate the thyroid gland, and thereby release the proper amount of thyroid hormones. This ensures that the growth process in young people is maintained and in some cases, even increased.

The four parathyroids embodied within the thyroid gland will start to function more effectively. They will work in harmony with—and complement—the thyroid. A parathyroid hormone (PTH) will be secreted in a proper amount into the bloodstream. Calcium and phosphate levels within the blood will be regulated. This in turn helps the kidneys to purify the blood more efficiently. As a whole, your energy level will increase when the thyroid and parathyroids are stimulated when performing the second set of chants.

The heart chakra is greatly affected by the second set of chants. As this energy center is activated, it opens up in a way similar to a flower opening to the newly risen sun. At the same time, the vibration created by this set of chants works into the upper part of the chest and causes the thymus gland to vibrate slightly. When the thymus gland vibrates, it activates and balances itself, allowing the proper amount of thyroid hormones to be produced. These hormones promote the proliferation and development of T cells, especially T3 and T4. These T cells destroy foreign microbes and substances. This is the key to a healthy immune system. A proper amount of thymic hormones being produced helps to slow down the aging process. Therefore, the second set of chants done in a prescribed manner can strengthen the thymus gland and its corresponding immune system and also profoundly slow down the aging of the body. The solar plexus chakra is very slightly affected by this set of chants as well.

The third and final set of chants of the Final Initiation influence the solar plexus, sacral plexus, and base chakras. On a physical level, the adrenals, the pancreas, and the reproductive organs are influenced. The vibration created by this set of chants works into these three organs causing them to vibrate or resonate slightly. This results in the adrenals, the pancreas, and the reproductive organs being stimulated somewhat.

The adrenals, two in number, sit atop the kidneys. They will release steroid hormones and sexual hormones into the body. The steroids are important for the maintenance of life. They maintain proper mineral balance in the blood and help to make you feel better, more balanced. The sexual hormones help to make you feel better and bring the energy level up.

If you suffer from a lack of libido, the release of sexual hormones will increase the sex drive. For those of you with a fairly normal sex drive, your libido will be maintained and even somewhat enhanced. This is true whether you are thirty or sixty years of age. A person can keep a strong, healthy sexual appetite for many years, right into his or her senior years.

Of course, if someone is oversexed, this final set of chants, done properly in the described musical note, will affect the already overactive sex drive. However, this effect will be very minimal and will only last for a very short time. In the long term, the adrenals that are releasing too many sexual hormones will start to adjust and balance themselves, resulting in a person with a high sex drive becoming more balanced and less sexually aroused. Thus the individual starts to develop a more healthy and regular sex drive.

If you can think back to a time when you were initially sexually attracted to someone and felt a warm feeling in your solar plexus, similar to a pleasant "butterflies in the stomach" sensation, then you were experiencing the solar plexus chakra being activated, as well as the adrenals. This was the steroid hormones and sexual hormones being released by these glands.

The adrenal glands are structurally divided into two regions. The adrenal cortex makes up the majority of the gland and surrounds the inner adrenal medulla. It is the adrenal cortex that is responsible for the release of both steroid hormones and sexual hormones.

The adrenal medulla, on the other hand, releases two hormones called epinephrine and norepinephrine. These secretions are commonly referred to as adrenalin and affect the central nervous system. In essence these secretions create a "fight or flight" response in a person if they are released in excessive amounts. When these two hormones are released in small amounts, a person feels energetic.

The third set of chants of the Final Initiation will profoundly affect the adrenal cortex and slightly influence the adrenal medulla. This allows a proper and necessary amount of hormones, including sex and steroid hormones, to be released into the bloodstream. These hormones will also affect both the central nervous system and the sympathetic nervous division, having a gently soothing effect on the nervous system. You may feel more relaxed, yet invigorated by this. On a higher vibrational level, the solar plexus chakra will not only be slightly activated by the chants, but will also open up somewhat. This allows for natural chi or Universal Energy to flow into this energy center thus allowing more healing vibrations to enter into the organs and tissues of this region of the body.

The pancreas, which is located slightly in front of and beside the stomach, will be activated by the third set of chants. This organ releases glucagon, insulin, and digestive enzymes. Glucagon is responsible for raising your blood glucose level in your body when this level falls below normal. The glucagon hormone targets the liver. It is here that this secretion accelerates the breakdown and conversion of amino acids and certain nutrients into glucose. A proper blood sugar or blood glucose level helps to maintain the body's metabolic rate.

Insulin has the opposite physiological action of glucagon. It helps to adjust the glucose level by decreasing the amount of glucose in the body when required. This important hormone is responsible for speeding up the transport of glucose into cells such as muscle fibers. It affects amino acids and also synthesizes proteins that are needed to maintain your health.

If toned properly during the third set of chants, the AME sound will help to balance the pancreas in such a way as to allow the right amounts of glucagon and insulin to be released into the bloodstream. This chanting should create a nice, pleasant vibration within the pancreas and the liver.

Many people may have improper or low amounts of digestive enzymes released by the pancreas. Due to the diet patterns and the addition of chemical supplements into the food chain, many people have an imbalance within this important organ, resulting in not enough of these enzymes being released for digestive purposes. The final set of chants will stimulate the pancreas to release more digestive enzymes. Incidentally, these enzymes, called peptides, are important in slowing down the aging process. In other words, digestive enzymes are one of the key secrets to long life!

The reproductive organs (testes in males, ovaries in females) start to become more harmonized after doing these chants. This results in more balanced secretions of either ovarian hormones (estrogens, progesterone) or testicular hormones (testosterone) into the body. A proper release of these respective sex hormones can help to maintain health and longevity.

For those who suffer from sexual dysfunctions, the third set of chants of the Final Initiation will alleviate some problems. For instance, a man with sexual impotence can sometimes reverse this frustrating condition by doing these chants in the prescribed manner. By combining this toning technique with certain chakra meditation exercises, some women may be able to slow down and lessen the less than positive aspects of menopause. Some of these chakra exercises were covered in detail in my book *Ancient Teachings for Beginners.* These same techniques or exercises will be discussed in even greater detail in chapter 7.

The Death Hormone

Medical science still does not know everything about the human body. This is especially true in regard to both the brain and the endocrine glandular system.

There are well over a hundred hormones that scientists have identified within our bodies. Each year more hormones or secretions are discovered. Eventually, the medical field will find and isolate a secretion that is partially responsible for greatly accelerating the human aging process. It is for this reason that it can be referred to as "the death hormone." This secretion is associated with the pituitary gland and the hypothalamus section of the brain.

The endocrine glandular system goes through subtle but important changes during the physiological breakdown of the body commonly known as the aging process. As previously stated, the release of human growth hormone (HGH) decreases significantly as you age. This in itself speeds up aging slightly. As HGH is released less and less through the years, other secretions and hormones become imbalanced and release improper levels into the bloodstream. The whole endocrine glandular system eventually becomes unbalanced. When this occurs, the death hormone starts to be released from within the pituitary and the hypothalamus section of the brain simultaneously. On a steady basis, the death hormone levels increase resulting in a faster breakdown of the human body. Thus a person starts to age rapidly at that point. You have all seen someone you know age in this manner. It almost seems as if this person has aged before your eyes.

Stress is one of the major culprits that can cause this hormone to be secreted into the body. A certain amount of stress may be good for you. Unfortunately our modern society has created much tension and extreme disharmony. For many people, a stressful world runs your lives. Deadlines must be met and life's pressures dealt with. As a consequence, too much stress affects your endocrine glandular system adversely, contributing to rapid aging.

The first set of chants of the Final Initiation, when done properly in the right musical note, will help to slow down the unwanted released of this hormone. In some cases, the first set of chants may even stop the release of the death hormone for a short period of time. In *Ancient Teachings for Beginners*, the MAY chant was described in detail. This particular chant can be used also to stop or slow down the release of this secretion.

Although the Final Initiation was designed as a one-time event in ancient times, it can be attempted on a semi-regular basis. Doing the three sets of chants on a monthly or even a bimonthly basis should prove beneficial for some people. It should be remembered that a universal intelligence comes into play. Finally your intuitive abilities and enhanced gifts determine when you should repeat this special initiation.

By combining these techniques along with other ones, you will ensure that you will receive positive results. When you do your own energy work on your chakras after initially completing this Final Initiation, the sensations within your body, your spine, and your chakras will be greatly enhanced.

Both chanting and chakra energy work contribute to a balanced endocrine system and an increase in psychic and spiritual abilities. You become healthy, whole, and balanced on all levels—mental, physical, and spiritual. Your true abilities will be fine-tuned, allowing you to function as a healer, teacher, or counselor.

> "Look within. Within is the fountain of good, and it will ever bubble up, if thou wilt ever dig."
> —Marcus Aurelius

Chapter 3

The Mind and the Brain

"The mind of man is capable of anything—because everything is in it, all the past as well as all the future."

—Joseph Conrad

As you become more enlightened, you start to use more of your brain's potential. Literally, your intelligence quotient will increase as new areas of your brain are awakened. At the same time, the power of your mind increases.

Most people think of the mind and the brain as one and the same thing. In reality, they are two separate and distinct creations.

The Difference Between the Mind and the Brain

People from all walks of life use the words "mind" and "brain" interchangeably. Doctors, scientists, and other highly trained people consider the mind and the brain as one and the same.

In reality, the brain is a biochemical organ, a part of the physical body. The mind, on the other hand, is a psychic "organ" that is attached to the human soul. Both the soul and the mind are connected to the Creator and the heavenly realms.

As human beings, we are dual in nature, possessing both a physical body and a psychic body. Within the physical body are physical organs and glands. Joined directly to the body is the psychic body, which contains psychic organs and glands. Both the physical and the psychic are linked so closely together that one does not function without the other's presence. For instance, the psychic heart resides within the physical heart. If there is a physiological problem within the actual physical heart, it will influence its psychic counterpart by creating a disharmony there. The psychic heart becomes slightly out of frequency or "sync" with the other psychic organs of the psychic body. This disharmony will also start to affect the physical heart by looping or feeding back from the psychic to the physical. If you can think of the feedback phenomenon in electronics, then you will have a general idea how this symbiotic relationship between the physical and psychic heart works. Even the human endocrine glandular system operates using a feedback or loop-back approach. Of course, all the physical organs and their respective psychic organs function under the same premise.

Now, when a physical organ such as the heart starts to lose its proper frequency, it becomes out of sync with the other physical organs and glands, resulting in disease. This can happen as a result of the psychic heart being out of sync or frequency as just stated, or some physical force may be the culprit. For instance, stress and worry may cause the physical heart to become diseased. If the physical heart, along with the psychic heart, both remain out of sync or off frequency, the situation will deteriorate to the point that perhaps major surgery, or even a heart transplant, becomes necessary.

Modern medicine is wonderful with all its miraculous procedures. However, medical science looks upon the human body in a purely mechanical and physical way. The psychic and the spiritual side of humankind are often overlooked. When a physical heart is removed from its host body, the psychic heart remains in place as part of the psychic body. As a healthy heart is transplanted in place of the just re-moved one, it is not connected in any way with the psychic heart that is resident within. This is one of the main reasons why many transplant recipients have rejection problems. Al-though, on a purely medical level, everything should match, the psychic body will not accept this physical organ at first. It takes awhile for the physical heart to become integrated with the recipient's psychic body.

When you possess an understanding of this just-men-tioned principle involving the physical and psychic nature of humankind, you will have a greater appreciation of en-ergy healing, which involves very high frequencies or rates of vibration.

The mind, a part of the human soul, has a profound influence upon the brain, the nervous system, the body, and all organs and glands. It is the mind that gives all of you the sense of cognition and sense of beingness.

The brain and the mind work in harmony with each other, the brain being the physical side and the mind the psychic side. This relationship allows the human body to maintain its health for a long period of time. The biochemical nature of your brain functions properly and automatically in a purely mechanical way because of this. Of course, this is a general statement and there are exceptions to this spiritual law as you are all aware. Brain abnormalities do exist, unfortunately.

As stated at the beginning of this chapter, you will use a greater amount of your mind power when you become more enlightened. This means that your mind as part of your eternal soul will connect to the heavenly fields and the Creator or Godsource much more easily. Attunement to the Divine Intelligence from the Creator above will become more readily available to you. Inspiration and wisdom from your angels and spirit guides will start to unfold on a regular basis. More light, higher vibrations of energy, such as Universal Energy, will enter into your soul and mind.

Also, this results in this high energy working into the physical brain and body, including, organs, glands, and cells. This is a step-down process. In other words, the high vibratory or light energy will enter into the eternal soul and mind first, and then into the physical form soon afterward. This energy steps down to a lower frequency.

This Divine Light or "Light of God" will go into the human aura and chakra system as well. This is why people who are spiritually and psychically advanced have very bright auras and large, clean chakras compared to most other individuals.

The Neocortex

On a physical level, the human brain will be affected in a special way as this high vibration of energy enters this organ. The brain consists of four principal parts, the brain stem, diencephalons (consisting of the thalamus and hypothalamus), cerebrum, and cerebellum (refer to figure 3.1, page 49). The Divine Light or Universal Energy will energize all areas and cause an electrical stimulation within. A part of the cerebrum that forms the bulk of the brain is particularly stimulated. This part is called the cerebral cortex or neocortex. This is the surface area of the cerebrum and is composed of gray matter two to four millimeters thick. Billions of neurons are contained in the neocortex. On an evolutionary scale, this is the most recently evolved or developed area of the human brain.

As the high vibration of energy or Divine Light works into this area and causes an electrical stimulation to occur, countless numbers of neurons start to fire. This firing of neurons will happen throughout some, or in many cases, all of the cerebral cortex or neocortex. (Incidentally, cortex means "rind" or "bark," and is aptly named.) This neuron-firing action will create a physiological sensation on the top of the head, or perhaps all over the head, sometimes referred to as "the tingles" because that is exactly what it will feel like to you. Obviously, if the neurons are firing throughout all or most of the neocortex, you as an initiated person will feel these tingles all over the head area where the crown chakra is located. Conversely, if only some neurons are firing near the top of the head, you will feel the tingling sensations only in this area.

For many people, this physiological sensation will be very intense and will feel as if a crown has been placed onto the head. This is one of the reasons why this chakra is referred to as the crown chakra.

This is a very special experience in regards to your spiritual growth and enlightenment. As the neurons fire they "open up" this area of the brain as well as some other areas. The cerebrum is considered the seat of intelligence, where higher processes of human thought exist. The ability to read, write, speak, and make calculations exists in this important part of the human brain. The creation of music, works of art, and philosophical thought originate from the cerebrum. In other words, some of your creative abilities are stored here. Always keep in mind that it is the *mind* as part of your eternal soul connected to the energy of the creator above that directs and allows those abilities to manifest on the physical level *via* the cerebrum.

Now, as these areas open up, Universal Energy or Divine Light, along with electrical energy, will enter these parts of the neocortex and cerebrum, stimulating brain cells that have lain dormant for a long time. These cells become active and start to perform their designated functions or tasks. As a human being you only use about 10 percent of your potential brain capacity. When the neurons fire and

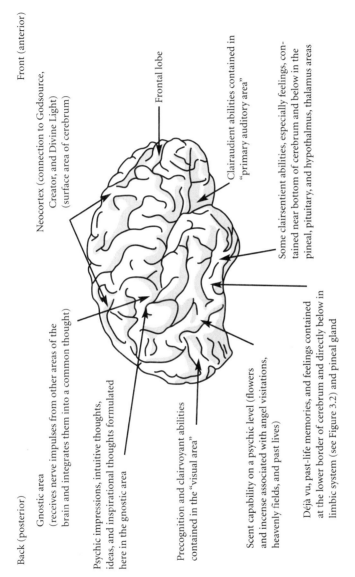

Back (posterior)

Front (anterior)

Gnostic area
(receives nerve impulses from other areas of the
brain and integrates them into a common thought)

Neocortex (connection to Godsource,
Creator, and Divine Light)
(surface area of cerebrum)

Frontal lobe

Clairaudient abilities contained in
"primary auditory area"

Psychic impressions, intuitive thoughts,
ideas, and inspirational thoughts formulated
here in the gnostic area

Some clairsentient abilities, especially feelings, contained near bottom of cerebrum and below in the
pineal, pituitary, and hypothalmus, thalamus areas

Precognition and clairvoyant abilities
contained in the "visual area"

Scent capability on a psychic level (flowers
and incense associated with angel visitations,
heavenly fields, and past lives)

Déjà vu, past-life memories, and feelings contained
at the lower border of cerebrum and directly below in
limbic system (see Figure 3.2) and pineal gland

Figure 3.1: The cerebrum (right lateral view), showing location
of psychic abilities.

these cells become activated, you start to use more of your mental or brain capacity. Thus, instead of using 10 percent, you increase your capacity to 20 or even 30 percent.

There are parts of the brain that contain psychic abilities such as precognition, déjà vu, past-life recall, clairaudience, and clairvoyance. As mentioned earlier, the cerebrum and the neocortex make up the majority of the brain. It is here that many of your psychic abilities are contained and merely lie dormant. The brain cells within these areas, when activated, will awaken these psychic attributes.

This is partly why spiritual enlightenment and divine inspiration occur when the crown chakra is opened and activated. Divine Light and wisdom enter into the crown area as well as energizing these areas of the brain.

As the Divine Light works through the cerebrum, it will also extend energy to other areas of the brain such as the pineal gland, pituitary gland, hypothalamus, and limbic system, including the thalamus. The pineal and pituitary are physical glands that possess a very psychic nature (see figure 3.1).

The majority of your intuitive faculties lie within the pineal gland. When it is activated by either a vibrational sound or Divine Light energy, this ability awakens in many people. For others who have this intuitive gift functioning already, it will be greatly enhanced. Also, past-life memories may awaken here, which in turn triggers more of these memories to be released from within the lower cerebrum and the thalamus. The thalamus is located directly above the pineal and pituitary-hypothalamus area of the brain.

These glands and specific areas work together in harmony to complete the full experience or memory of a past-life event. All are necessary much the same as each instrument in an orchestra is necessary to create beautiful music.

The pituitary gland, being of a spiritual as well as psychic nature, has a close connection to the higher energies associated with the Creator and the heavenly fields. Divine inspiration, spiritual enlightenment, and a closer affinity to angels and heaven may be the results when the pituitary is stimulated and activated.

The hypothalamus will be greatly affected by the activation of either or both of these special glands. Past-life emotions directly associated with past-life memories may arise here as the Divine Energy and vibrations work into the hypothalamus.

If you refer to figure 3.2 on page 52, you will notice an area of the cerebrum associated with smells of a psychic nature. This includes the scent of smoke, incense, or other odors during the recall of a previous lifetime. Certain individuals will experience this as very real. This happens when this area of the cerebrum is stimulated before or during a past-life remembrance. There is one other area of the brain that is activated and works in conjunction with this part of the cerebrum, and will be discussed shortly.

The Limbic System

The limbic system is situated directly below the cerebrum, and contains the thalamus, hippocampus, and olfactory bulb. As shown in the illustration, the hippocampus contains

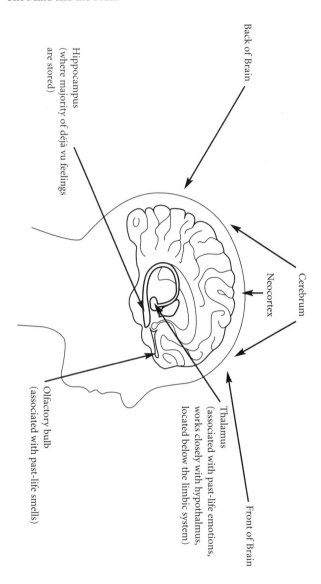

Back of Brain

Hippocampus
(where majority of déjà vu feelings are stored)

Cerebrum

Neocortex

Olfactory bulb
(associated with past-life smells)

Thalamus
(associated with past-life emotions, works closely with hypothalmus, located below the limbic system)

Front of Brain

Figure 3.2: Limbic system, where déjà vu and some past-life memories and feelings are stored. Please note it works in conjunction with the lower border of cerebrum and the pineal, pituitary, and hypothalamus areas to create past-life recall.

the feelings associated with déjà vu. An electrical stimulation, or even a vibration, directed through here can trigger powerful impressions or feelings of déjà vu.

The olfactory bulb, situated closer toward the front of the brain near the frontal lobe, is the main area associated with past-life smells. It does, however, work together with an area of the cerebrum situated more toward the back of the brain. The stimulation and activation of either or both of these areas will create psychic smells.

As mentioned before, the thalamus works closely with the pineal and pituitary glands and the hypothalamus, in regard to past-life memories. In conjunction with the hypothalamus, the thalamus brings past-life emotions to the surface, too. As parts of the limbic system, the hippocampus and the thalamus are in close proximity to one another. This closeness ensures that déjà vu feelings and past-life memories and emotions have some similarities.

Psychic abilities (such as clairvoyance, precognition, clairaudience, clairsentience, and psychic impressions) lie within the cerebrum. Intuition and creativity are mostly contained within the pineal and pituitary, respectively. These glands influence the cerebrum in such a way as to heighten the intuitive and creative faculties.

Although the human brain is divided into left and right hemispheres, with the left hemisphere being considered the logical side, and the right one the creative side, both hemispheres contain psychic and spiritual abilities. As an initiated person, you will use both hemispheres of your brain more effectively when the neocortex and cerebrum have been stimulated. If you have been left-brain oriented for a long time, you will notice that you are starting to use the right side more often, and vice versa. This is all part of being spiritually enlightened and advanced.

"No man is free who is not master of himself."

—Epictetus

In chapters 1 and 2, the Final Initiation was described in detail. It is the first set of chants of this ancient initiation that affects the crown and third eye chakras. Of course, the pineal, pituitary, and hypothalamus are greatly affected by this AME chant performed in a high-to-mid-C musical note. Other areas of the brain, such as the neocortex, cerebrum, and the limbic system, which includes the thalamus and hippocampus, are all profoundly affected, too. The more receptive you are to energy, the better the results. This is the case for all who are initiated and advanced.

In my previous book *Ancient Teachings for Beginners,* a special chant was given in order to create a vibration within the pituitary and awaken the crown chakra. This MAY chant, done in a mid-C musical note about two to three times, also helped to awaken the neocortex and stimulate dominant areas of the cerebrum. The thalamus and other areas of the limbic system would also be affected by performing this vibrational chant.

This special chant will be discussed briefly as a review for some readers, and for the benefit of those who have not read the previous book. For simplicity's sake, any techniques or exercises found within the following pages that originated from *Ancient Teachings for Beginners* will be covered in detail. Some of these techniques will be expansions or continuations of the original ones. Many of the exercises and techniques will be completely new to you. Therefore a continued reference to the first book will not be necessary in most cases.

The Crown Chakra Chant

First, relax yourself by taking a breath deep into your lungs and diaphragm, holding it for about five to ten seconds. It is important to draw air into *all* of your lungs, not just the upper part of the lungs. Then, release your breath slowly and evenly, either through your nose or mouth. This is your choice. Now, take in another deep breath and repeat the process. Do it once again with a third and final deep breath. When you do deep breathing for three times and hold the breath in, the chi or Universal Energy contained around you in the air is drawn into your lungs. As this breath containing the chi is held within, it helps to expand and cleanse your auric field. Your brain wave patterns will slow down, allowing you to enter into a more relaxed state.

Now, take in one more deep breath, hold it for a few seconds, and then begin to release it. As you do, chant M-M-A-A-Y-Y evenly and strongly until your breath is completely exhaled. This chant should be attempted in a mid-C musical note, approximately. If you are not musically inclined, do not worry. Simply find a sound or scale not too high and not too low, but in between, a mid-point. Repeat the MAY chant once more, letting yourself feel the vibration working

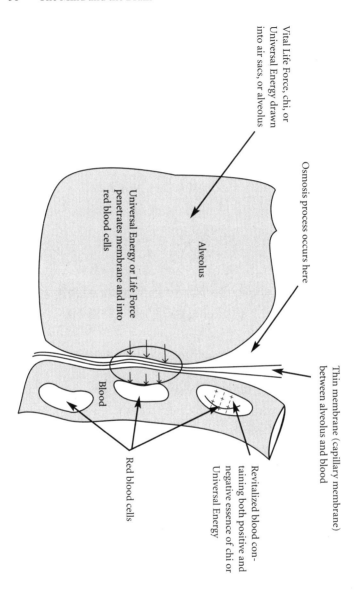

Figure 3.3: Alveolus, containing air sacs or chambers, separated from blood (red blood cells) by thin membrane.

from your third eye or brow area and into the middle of the head, and finally up toward the top of your head where the crown chakra is located. Repeat this a third and final time, allowing the sound to work throughout the head. For many, you will feel "the tingles" on the top of the head or other parts of the head. Some of you will feel lightheaded. These are indications that the pituitary gland and surrounding areas of the brain are being affected. The crown chakra then opens up, allowing you access to the Creator or Godsource.

The Chi Deep-Breathing Exercise

The deep-breathing exercise just explained to you, although simple to do, starts an amazing process in the human body. It is important that three deep breaths are taken in, held for about five to ten seconds, and then slowly released. Three is a magical and mystical number. Three represents completion, and involves the Law of Three or the Law of the Triangle (see figure 3.4).

This law is in direct reference to the chi or Universal Energy that is everywhere, that surrounds you, and is in the air that you breathe. It also involves reincarnation and the Holy Trinity. These two subjects will be reviewed in a later chapter.

The chi or Universal Energy (also called Life Force) held in your breath consists of two elements, positive essence and negative essence. This is based on the same principle as the Law of Magnetism and the Law of Electricity. Both the negative and positive elements or polarities are important

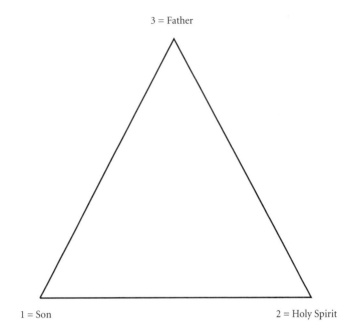

1 = Positive Polarity Energy
2 = Negative Polarity Energy
3 = Combination of 1 and 2 is Universal Energy,
chi, or Life Force

Figure 3.4: The Holy Trinity: Father, Son, and Holy Spirit originate from the Law of Three or the Law of the Triangle.

and of equal value. One needs the other and they work in harmony together.

When you take a deep breath into your lungs, the air, consisting of this Life Force, enters into little cup-shaped pouches called alveoli. There are air sacs or chambers within these alveoli (alveolus, singular). When the heart sends the depleted blood containing red blood cells into the lungs by way of capillaries, they pass by the alveoli, which now contain the Universal Energy or chi. A very thin membrane separates both. Through the process of osmosis, the chi, or Life Force, consisting of both positive and negative essence, enters into the blood cells. Divine Intelligence is involved in all of this. As a part of this, the red blood cells possess their own form of this intelligence. Each cell needs a certain amount of positive and negative elements. Some cells will need equal portions of both polarities, others will need more positive energy and less negative energy. Through the power of the human mind and Divine Intelligence, each red blood cell as an individual will draw in the proper amount of positive and negative polarities or essences of the Universal Energy, or chi.

It is through this process of osmosis that this amazing transference occurs. Most of the cells will absorb 50 percent positive elements. In some cases, specific cells require 70 percent positive energy and 30 percent negative energy or vice versa. This is where the ancient Chinese philosophy of Yin and Yang comes into play. A proper balance of both is needed.

It is through the process of proper deep breathing, along with specific breath holding techniques, that your lungs draw in the required amount of Life Force or Universal Energy needed to revitalize and sustain your physical form. Practicing the Chi Deep-Breathing Exercise on a daily basis greatly assists in slowing down the aging process. When you hold your breath for a period of five to ten seconds, more chi or Life Force is released into the blood cells, which in turn take it through the circulatory system and into the cells, tissues, glands, and organs of the body. It is important that the breath be held deep in your lungs for at least five seconds or more to ensure that each individual blood cell is fully "charged" with this Universal Energy. This will ensure that the Life Force is transported to every part of your body with maximum potential. In turn, the chi energy will also be released from the organs and glands of the physical form into the chakra system and auric field, as well. Thus, your chakras become lighter and your human energy field or aura expands and brightens.

This is the goal that an initiated person strives to attain. When your auric field is bright, expanded and strong, and your energy centers or chakras are clean and light, you affect people around you. Your expanded auric field will radiate light and energy out toward individuals near you, making them feel better and calmer. This energy is subtle but effective.

Truly gifted teachers, counselors, and healers possess bright, powerful auras that influence people. These enlightened people use the infinite power of the human mind to help humanity.

> "The light of heaven and the wisdom of the Creator can be found in everyone."
>
> —Douglas De Long

Chapter 4

Creative Mind Power

"All that we are is the result of what we have thought; it is founded on our thoughts and made up of our thoughts. If a man speaks or acts with an evil thought, suffering follows him as a wheel follows the hoof of a beast that draws the cart."

—Dhammapada

The power of the human mind is great. In this chapter we will discuss some special techniques to enhance your mind potential and creative abilities.

As you become more spiritually enlightened, you develop a power to create and manifest things and events in your life quickly. This is due to the fact that you are using more of your brain and ultimately your mind, which directs it. If you possess negative or unhealthy thoughts in either your conscious or subconscious mind, you can influence your desires and wishes in a way that is not beneficial to you.

There are two metaphysical laws or principles involved in all of this. The first one is called the Law of Four.

The Law of Four

Number and geometric patterns have been used for countless centuries throughout the world as symbols. Symbology can sometimes hide secrets.

The Law of Four, also referred to as the Law of the Square, holds great mystical significance. The number four has connections to many sacred truths and hidden knowledge. As an advanced spiritual person, you should have an understanding of this law or principle.

First of all, this law should be looked at in a historical and mystical perspective. The number four represents the four elements: air, water, fire, and earth. All of these four elements are important to anyone on a spiritual path. The use of symbology and sacred numbers can be found worldwide in different cultures and religions. The number four is an important aspect of this.

Native Peoples of North America

For many of the native peoples of North America, such as the Cree and the Sioux, the number four refers to the four directions. North, south, east, and west are indicated by the four colors white, black, red, and yellow, respectively, in the Sioux tradition. For the Cree nation, blue is used in place of black. Even the Apache belief is similar with the four colors of white, blue, black, and yellow representing north, south, east, and west.

This concept brings us to the next important belief. These colors in their various arrangements are also symbols for the four races of Earth: white, black, red, and yellow. When all four races, white (Caucasian), red (Native American), yellow (Asian), and black (Negroid) become more spiritual and work together as one, our world will become a heaven on Earth. Spiritual enlightenment and peace will be the result.

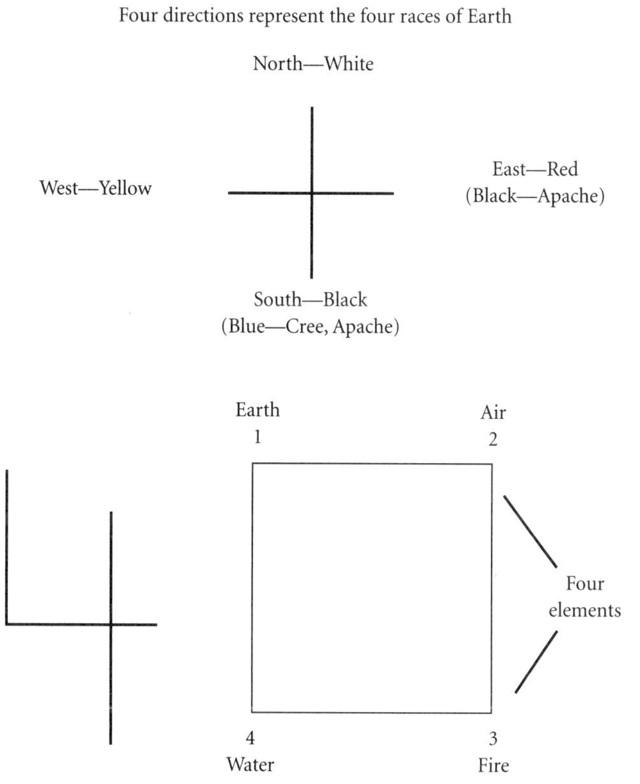

Four directions represent the four races of Earth

North—White

West—Yellow

East—Red
(Black—Apache)

South—Black
(Blue—Cree, Apache)

Earth
1

Air
2

Four
elements

4
Water

3
Fire

Four corners of the square also refer to the four corners or base of pyramid

Figure 4.1: Significance of the Law of Four or Law of the Square.

On another note, the number four in the Cree culture represents the number of days needed before a deceased person is buried. Four days is directly associated with the time needed for a human soul to completely depart the body and return to the universe. This indicates that four is a sacred number as well.

Christian Mysticism

The number four holds a special, spiritual significance for Christian mystics. This number refers to the crucifixion wounds of Jesus, the Master Teacher. The wounds on both wrists count as one, the wounds of both ankles as two, the crown of thorns makes three, and the spear wound in Jesus' side is four. In this case, four represents an end or completion of one event, the crucifixion. Of course, in the Christian faith this event is followed by the resurrection.

Jewish Mysticism and the Kabala

The Jewish religion is very mystical in nature. All forms of Judaism can be said to hold mystical beliefs that describe how to achieve communion with the Godsource. Many ideas related to this can be found in written works. The teachings within these writings form the Kabala (a word meaning "tradition"). The Kabala is an esoteric form of Jewish mysticism recorded in several ancient and medieval books, two of the most well-known of these are the Zohar and the Sepher Yezirah.

The Zohar, or "Book of Splendor," was written in the thirteenth century, while the Sepher Yezirah, or "Book of

Creation," was written between the third and sixth centuries B.C.E. It is in the earlier writings, the "Book of Creation," that the number four is shown as a representation of the four elements: earth, air, fire, and water. These ancient texts also mention that the number four symbolizes the four directions, north, south, east, and west. This fits in with other beliefs about the number four, the elements and the four directions.

The Sepher Yezirah goes one step further and states that the number four also refers to four important metals: gold, silver, copper, and iron. These examples indicate the importance of the number four and how they can relate to the Law of Four or the Law of the Square.

This brings us to the next important part of the Law of Four or the Law of the Square. Four represents the power of the human mind to create or manifest something. It is actually the completion of the manifestation process. In this case the number four refers to the following four things: the human mind, which controls the brain and is linked to the eternal soul, has the conscious mind, the subconscious mind, the superconsciousness, and the Divine Intelligence as parts of its special makeup. The conscious mind consists of your waking thoughts, ideas, and cognitive abilities. For most people, this is reality.

The subconscious mind, on the other hand, consists of buried thoughts, beliefs, and concepts; even fears are hidden here. These all exist just below the conscious mind and can influence you. Many people have little or no awareness of some of the things buried or hidden within the recesses of the subconscious.

The superconsciousness is a part of your mind that is connected to Divine Intelligence or Universal Wisdom. It is this Universal Wisdom, as part of a collective consciousness, that is directly associated with the heavenly fields and the Creator, or Godsource. It is here that the knowledge and wisdom from above can be tapped into and accessed by the human mind.

> "Wisdom makes her sons exalted, and lays hold of those that seek her. Whoever loves her, loves life, and those who seek her early will be filled with joy."
>
> —Ben Sira

The Law of Creation or Manifestation

This brings us to the next phase that is closely associated with the Law of Four. This metaphysical principle is called the Law of Creation, or the Law of Manifestation. It works in conjunction with the just-mentioned four aspects of the human mind.

The conscious and subconscious minds are very important in regard to creating or manifesting things or events that you desire. It is essential that these two parts of the mind work together in harmony. For many individuals, conflict exists between the conscious and subconscious. This in itself creates problems for anyone trying to use mind power to manifest something. At best, the results can be less than desirable. In many cases, nothing may come from the attempt.

There are many schools of thought regarding how to create or manifest desires or wants. All are based on positive thoughts and aspirations. One of the key concepts involves focusing. However, before attempting any focusing techniques, the conflicts between your conscious and subconscious mind must be resolved.

Many people walk around with deep-seated pain, anger, and negative thoughts contained within both of these parts of their mind. Negative thoughts, both on a conscious and subconscious level, can create havoc, disharmony, and unpleasantness in a person's life. If these thoughts and negative beliefs remain unchecked, an unhappy, miserable life may ensue. This will eventually lead to physical problems within the body. Poor health and early death may be the ultimate results of continued long-term negative thinking. This is not to say that all illness is due to a negative frame of mind. There are countless reasons for the human body to break down with serious health conditions, but negativity is a great contributor to poor health and also lack of abundance in life.

For many on a spiritual path, this is one of the first things you would have recognized and started to change for the better. Even your actions and spoken words would have changed accordingly. Positive thoughts, actions, and spoken words would be part of the spirituality that you now embrace. Thinking, acting, and speaking in a more positive manner affects the conscious mind by making proper changes to the thought process. This influences the brain on a physical level, allowing it to function more effectively with heightened brain activity. Intuition, creativity, and clarity become stronger. Greater amounts of endorphins, including serotonin, are released by the brain and brain stem into the bloodstream. This will give you a sense of aliveness and contentment. In other words, positive thoughts and words create positive feelings within.

The longer you continue to think in this way, the more the positive thoughts influence your conscious mind by replacing negative thoughts and ideas. When this happens, even the auric field around you changes for the better. The aura starts to look brighter and cleaner, especially about the crown chakra area and all of the head.

Conscious thought patterns start to change from negative to positive ways instantly, in some cases. Merely thinking or saying the proper thought or words begins the desired change. However, in some circumstances, unhealthy thought patterns on a conscious level take some time to be erased and replaced with healthy, positive thoughts. This process may take anywhere from a week to several months to fully integrate into the consciousness.

When some of the positive patterns become accepted as part of the conscious mind, it will begin to influence the subconscious mind like streaks of light entering a dark cave. Once the conscious mind functions completely in a productive, healthy way, it will influence the subconscious even more effectively.

Eventually the subconscious mind with all its dark recesses will become brighter. The negativity residing here will lessen as more positive thoughts become entrenched within. It is at this point that the aura becomes even cleaner in appearance. The conflict that may have existed between these two parts of your mind has been removed. A major block to your creative potential no longer exists.

There are certain techniques or exercises you can employ to speed up these changes to both the conscious and subconscious minds. The first of these is the Conscious Mind Focusing Exercise.

Conscious Mind Focusing Exercise

In regards to the conscious level, specific positive affirmations can be thought about, focused on, and then spoken out loud in a normal voice. Pick out three to five affirmations that you wish to use. If you try to work with more than five affirmations at a time, the results may be not as powerful and expedient as it would be with a lesser amount.

As an example, you could try the following three together: peace of mind, health and happiness. These three key expressions would be used in the following manner. Place them into very short sentences. These would then read as, *"I have peace of mind, I am healthy, and I am filled with happiness."*

Once you have decided upon the positive affirmations you will use, start to think about them several times during the day. Focus all your attention on these three to five thoughts for several moments. All of your mental energy should be directed towards this. Your ability to concentrate and focus specifically on something for a short period of time trains your mind for creative vocalization. A focused mind has great power and helps you to manifest circumstances and physical things in your life.

Now, during the day you should also say these affirmations in a clear, normal voice. For example, *"I have peace of mind," "I am healthy,"* and *"I am filled with happiness!"* If you say these affirmations three or four times a day it should be sufficient. Sometimes, you can even think these thoughts and voice them out loud at the same time. You do not have to yell; a firm yet quiet voice is fine.

All of this should be attempted when you are in a full waking state. This is referred to as the beta state and occurs in most people when they are awake and working. These brain wave patterns operate at a faster frequency of, or more than, fourteen cycles per second (cps) or hertz (Hz). These patterns are associated with the conscious mind for most people.

However, when you are more spiritually awakened or enlightened, you do not operate as often in the beta level. Although you are wide awake and working at your prescribed employment, your brain wave patterns will operate at a slower pace or frequency. Technically, you may be in a light altered state of consciousness. This is called the alpha state and the brain waves or rhythms operate between eight and thirteen cycles per second (Hz).

This is all right. The process of positive change will still unfold. In fact, the change may be even faster for you.

The Conscious Mind Focusing Exercise should be employed for about twenty-one days. This ensures that the conscious thought patterns become very healthy and beneficial in a relatively short period of time. This exercise works into the subconscious mind to a lesser degree, as well.

The Conscious-to-Subconscious Mind-Link Exercise

You are now ready to do the next important exercise that involves the power of your mind.

This particular technique should be employed at bedtime, just prior to falling asleep. This time of day is best because both your mind and body are at rest. Your brain wave rhythms will likely be in a light to medium alpha state. This allows the conscious and subconscious to become in tune with each other. When this happens, it is easier for the conscious mind to release thoughts, ideas, and impressions into your subconscious.

Before you begin, think of five to ten concepts or positive affirmations. Write them down as well. Some of these thoughts should be of a spiritual nature. For instance, peace of mind and spiritual harmony are two good examples that you might consider. Now, look at the list that you have created. Read it over several times, either mumbling the words under your breath or thinking them in your head. Do this until you have memorized your affirmation list. Once you have reached this point, you can now employ the Conscious-to-Subconscious Mind-Link Exercise just prior to falling asleep. Make sure that you are very relaxed and in a comfortable position. Do some deep breathing, about three or four times. This will help you to become even more restful.

Now, start focusing on your memorized list. Mumble the words once under your breath and then think about each affirmation or concept, letting yourself go through the list. Continue doing this over and over again as you get more relaxed and closer to slumber. Then, let yourself fall asleep.

Several things happen as you enter into the slumber state. First of all, the brain wave rhythms will slow down. When lying in a relaxed state, your brain wave patterns will be in a light alpha state which is below fourteen cycles per second or Hz. As you continued to relax and do your deep breathing, these patterns or rhythms would have slowed down to about eight cycles per second, which puts you into a medium-to-deep alpha state.

Upon falling asleep, the brain wave rhythms slow down even more. This is the theta state, and the brain wave rhythms are below seven cycles per second. As you fall deeper into sleep, your brain wave patterns enter into the delta state, which has an approximate frequency of three to four cycles per second.

Notice that these are four states of consciousness consisting of the beta, alpha, theta, and delta brain wave rhythms. This, of course, is in conjunction with the Law of Four or the Law of the Square.

As stated, when your brain wave patterns are in the light alpha state, the conscious and subconscious begin to link to one another. This allows thoughts from your conscious mind to be released into your subconscious mind.

As the brain waves continue to slow down, the connection between these two aspects of your mind becomes stronger. This ensures that these affirmations you memorized and concentrated on work into the subconscious.

The theta level has a deep connection with the subconscious mind. Your positive thoughts and ideas from the conscious level will start to become ingrained deep in the recesses of the subconscious. Soon, the thoughts and affirmations that you have memorized become part of both your conscious and subconscious thoughts and beliefs.

When you are in a delta or theta brain wave pattern, your conscious and subconscious minds will also connect with the superconsciousness. This special part of your mind connects to the Divine Intelligence or Universal Wisdom that comes directly from the heavenly fields and the Creator. While in this sleeping state, you will access knowledge, wisdom, and information that is important to you and your spiritual growth. In many cases, your spirit guides and angels communicate with you here and pass on messages.

When you are spiritually awakened, you access more information and remember a great deal of knowledge while in these sleeping states. You are able to retrieve more of this wisdom and knowledge than someone who is not spiritually awakened or enlightened. This is a special teaching method that your spirit helpers may use to assist you with your life.

While in a delta or theta state, you will also soul travel easily. It is during these times that you will visit teaching temples and other wonderful places in the heavenly fields.

Your spirit guides and angels will teach you and guide you up here in these special places while you are in your soul body.

The Conscious-to-Subconscious Mind-Link Exercise should be practiced every night for a period of seven to ten days. This amount of time ensures that you will receive the most benefit from this mind exercise. Within a month of completing this technique, your subconscious mind will be more positive in nature and be in harmony with the conscious, waking state. You may feel different at this point. In many situations, you will feel lighter, happier, and more balanced in life. Some might feel a sense of peace or contentment within.

This exercise can be tried again every three to four months, approximately. Of course, the next time that you try it, create a new and different list of positive affirmations and spiritual thoughts. If you make a habit of practicing this exercise over the years, your conscious and subconscious minds will become more positive, harmonious, and more enlightened. You will develop incredible mind power.

The Law of Creation Exercise

You are now fully ready to employ the most powerful and important exercise associated with the power of your mind! As an initiated person, you use more of your brain capacity and ultimately your mind that directs it. This means that you have more control over your life and the events that surround it.

A spiritually enlightened person must be careful in regard to thoughts, words, and actions. As you think, so you create. When you use more of your brain capacity, you have the ability to create or manifest more things and events into your life. You will also do this in a very quick manner compared to someone that is less open and spiritual.

With that in mind, the Law of Creation Exercise will now be explained to you in detail. There are certain key conditions that must be observed when you do this. Under the Law of Creation, the desired goal or object must not be based on pure greed and selfishness. The desired result should not hurt or interfere with another human being. Your ultimate desire should be used for both the greater good for you and someone else. If several people can benefit from this desire manifesting, then the chances of success are greater.

This technique, like the Conscious-to-Subconscious Mind-Link Exercise, works best at nighttime just prior to falling asleep. It can also be tried during the day if you can allow yourself to enter into a deep altered state of consciousness. Of course, this would mean that your brain wave patterns are deep within the alpha state.

Once you are very relaxed, either prior to falling asleep or in a deep meditative state, you should use the following focusing and visualization method. First of all, think of something in your life at this moment that you would like to change for the better. You can also think about something that does not exist in your life, but which you would like to have.

You may use the subsequent examples if you want. Some of you who are spiritually awakened may be searching for your true purpose in life. For many, you may be seeking a better job, one that is better suited to your life and beliefs. For others, your purpose or path in life is clear and you are doing your intended work. However, business and opportunities are slow, if not lacking, as you struggle toward your goals.

With the three just-mentioned situations, the following method should be used to make the desired changes. There will be slight variations with each unique situation, but the general technique will work well for all.

If you are seeking your life's purpose, mentally ask your angels and spirit guides to help you to find answers or signposts, while your mind and body are deeply relaxed.

This is the ideal time to communicate and work with these beings of light. You are more receptive and in tune with guides and angels during this altered state of consciousness.

With unspoken words, express what you truly desire and ask them to open the doors for you. Feel the emotions of gratitude and happiness coming to the surface. Enjoy these sensations for a few moments. Finally, in your mind say, "As I ask, I shall receive." Then let this thought go with the knowledge that all will unfold as it should. Let yourself drift off to sleep at this point, or if you are meditating, just let your mind wander for a while. Repeat this exercise in the same manner the next day. Do this technique once again for a third day. Then try it again a fourth and final day. By doing this exercise once a day for four consecutive days, you are employing the Law of Four. This guarantees the greatest chance of success.

For those seeking a better job with a future, employ the Law of Creation Exercise in the following manner. Firstly, ask your angels and spirit guides to help you in creating the ideal position for you at this time in your life. Ask them and the Creator above to grant you a fruitful and positive future.

Now, imagine yourself meeting a potential employer during a job interview. See yourself shaking hands with this individual as he or she offers you the wonderful position and congratulates you. Let the sensation of confidence come forth. Feel the emotions of joy, contentment, and happiness. Experience it as happening right now. Enjoy these sensations for a few moments. Then repeat the phrase, "As I ask, I shall receive." Then allow yourself to fall asleep or just drift if you are meditating. As stated before, do this exercise for four consecutive days.

In regard to the third example of wanting to increase your business that pertains to your purpose in life, change the exercise just slightly. For instance, if you work as an energy healer, such as a Reiki practitioner, ask the Creator and your angels and spirit helpers to assist in bringing more clients or patients to you. In your mind, ask that the right people come to see you for treatments. Visualize these people calling you, and see and sense them in your treatment room, whether it is in your home or in an office.

Feel the emotions of happiness and gratitude. Experience the sense of fulfillment associated with helping people who need your services. Let it feel very real, as if it is happening right this moment. Enjoy these sensations for a few moments. Then, as in the other two examples, say in your mind, "As I ask, I shall receive." Allow yourself to enter into sleep, or just let your mind wander if you are in meditation.

These are but three examples you can use. Obviously, if you desire something else, whether it is of a physical or spiritual nature, the same approach can be used. Simply adjust the exercise to fit the need. Use your creativity and imagination in order to manifest what you truly need and desire. Make sure that you do follow the general guidelines.

After completing your customized version of the Law of Creation Exercise, just go about your normal business. Forget about what you focused on in this special manifestation exercise. Do not dwell on these thoughts. The reason for this is simple. If you continue to focus on these thoughts, they will remain within your mind and will not be released. So let them go!

This will allow the desired thoughts and wishes to be released into the universe. These thoughts are real and form into an energy pattern that vibrates at a very high frequency or cycles per second (Hz).

When you let these ideas and desires go, they work similar to radio waves in electronics. If you can think of an FM radio station sending its radio signals out into the air and then being picked up by countless radio receivers, then you will understand how this process works.

This energy pattern will radiate from your brain and mind outward. This "signal" will be received on a spiritual and psychic level by people who are receptive to this energy. As your thought vibrations are released from your mind, your angels and spirit guides assist with the process. These beings of light will open doors for you by creating certain events or situations that bring you closer to your desires that you focused on. Also, in a gentle and unobtrusive way, your spirit guides and angels will communicate with and influence these certain people to help you. This is subtle but effective.

Some of these individuals will feel an urge or compulsion to assist you. They may not know why, but nevertheless they will help at the right moment in your life. Others may experience an even stronger urge or knowing that they need to assist you in some way. In some cases this may come to the person as a message from their angels and spirit guides, or perhaps information and insight will be given to them during a dream or meditation. This is how angels and spirit guides help in many ways.

Also, the energy that was created by your focused and then released thoughts will be received by the subconscious mind as you drift asleep. This enforces the desires and thoughts deep within your being.

It was mentioned earlier that four aspects comprise the makeup of the human mind: the conscious, the subconscious, the superconscious, and Divine Intelligence. The latter is also referred to as the Divine Mind where universal wisdom exists.

As you enter into sleep, your subconscious connects with the superconscious mind as well. It is here that wonderful things happen. This superconsciousness or "higher mind" is actually a part of the Divine Mind. Consider it as a single drop in an ocean of wisdom. This ocean is vast and universal, and is an aspect of the Creator and heavenly fields above. The superconscious mind will gather knowledge, wisdom, insight, and information from this Divine Intelligence or Divine Mind. It will then pass this assimilated information on to your subconscious mind during sleep. Some of this will be in the form of answers or direction that you need. During your waking states, these answers will come to your mind when you least expect them through visions and intuitive impressions.

This process also works two ways. Your thoughts and desires will enter into the superconscious and ultimately the Divine Mind above which contains all. These desires take the form of energy here, vibrating at an extremely high frequency. It resonates with this Divine Intelligence. With its infinite wisdom, this part of the Godsource or Creator allows this energy to expand outward where it begins the manifestation process. This may unfold in wondrous yet mysterious ways. Perhaps synchronicity will become even more apparent in your life. For instance, the right things may come to you at the right time. Your life will start to flow more effortlessly and harmoniously, too. Do not question it. Just simply let it be.

If you are practicing the Law of Creation Exercise using the meditation approach, the results will be the same, but take longer to accomplish. In this case, the conscious mind will be involved with the whole process. It has a slight tendency to rationalize everything, thus slowing things down somewhat. However, this approach is still powerful and effective.

Once you have completed this special exercise, allow yourself to go about your normal, everyday affairs for the next few weeks. During this period of time, it is important that you do not worry excessively or let yourself become angry too often. If you do you will block or interfere with the manifestation process. So try to remain relatively calm and settled.

Finally, when certain events and situations start to unfold, you must follow up with action on your part. For example, you may have recently applied to what you believe to be the ideal job. You may have just received a phone call from your prospective employer informing you that you are "short-listed" for the position. It is now between you and two other candidates. It is at this point that you must show up for the final interview with a positive attitude. Let your intuition guide you as you answer questions while you present yourself in a clear and honest manner. Be yourself. This, obviously, will increase your chances of success.

Whether you are actually offered the position or not is not as relevant as the following point. Realize that you have used the power of your mind in a powerful way to create the ideal situation. When you continue to use your mind in this positive manner, more of these opportunities will come into your life. In some cases, physical objects that you want and need will manifest for you as well.

Under the Law of Creation, the greater the desire, the longer it takes to come to fruition. In other words, some smaller desires or goals may begin to manifest in a few days. Some will take several weeks. Others, such as a life-changing event, may take several months to manifest.

The more you use your creative abilities as an initiated person, the more fulfilling your life will become. You are a spark of the Divine Light.

> "Riches are not from abundance of worldly goods, but from a contented mind."
>
> —Muhammad

Chapter 5

Ancient Healing Techniques

"There is a light that shines beyond all things
on earth, beyond us all, beyond the heavens,
beyond the highest, the very highest heavens.
This is the Light that shines in our heart."

—Chandogya Upanishad

In ancient times, humankind understood the relationship
between the physical and spiritual to a far greater depth
than society does today. Fortunately, all this is changing.
Millions of people worldwide are exploring and delving
into the ancient mysteries. Much of this involves the healing techniques practiced by our ancestors.

The Master Jesus is a prime example of someone who
was thoroughly familiar with all of this. He taught many disciples and followers, including women, these ancient mysteries and healing techniques.

In this chapter, ancient healing techniques will be covered in detail. Some of the information will be of a basic nature. However, the majority of the techniques discussed will involve more advanced principles. As an initiated and spiritually opened person, you will be able to utilize all of the techniques.

All of you possess your own innate healing abilities. This healing potential within can be tapped into in order to help yourself and others.

Nerve Meridians and Energy Meridians

There are nerve meridians that run throughout the whole body. The ends of some of these meridians can be found at the ends of the toes, thumbs, and fingers. These meridians contain a "nerve energy" that works into the body for healing purposes. This energy helps to maintain health and allows vitality to flow throughout your entire physical form.

The spinal column contains all of this nerve energy and releases it into the human nervous system, which includes all of the nerve meridians that branch off from the spine. The spinal column itself consists of the Central Nervous System running down through the center. Impulses and signals flow up and down through the Central Nervous System, from the brain down to the feet.

Along both sides of the Central System is the Sympathetic Nervous Division, or SND. The Parasympathetic Division exists here, also within these two trunks (see figure 5.1).

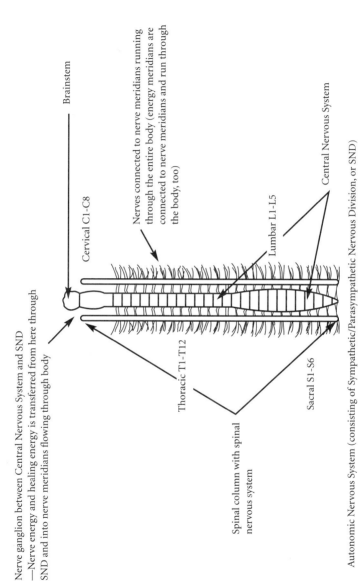

Figure 5.1: Spinal column, the Central Nervous System, Sympathetic Nervous Division, and healing energy and nerve energy.

The nerve energy is released from the Central Nervous System into ganglia, which are collections of nerves. These ganglia are situated up and down the spine between the Central System and the SND. Contained within these ganglia and the Sympathetic Nervous Division is another type of energy, a healing energy that vibrates at a very high frequency. This energy is part of the Divine Energy or Universal Energy that exists all around you and is also present in the heavenly fields above. It is often times referred to as chi or prana. Everyone has this special healing energy within. In a way, it is your part of the divine. When released this energy can heal in a miraculous manner.

Energy meridians exist within the physical form and, like nerve meridians, run through the whole body. These meridians begin at both trunks of the Sympathetic Nervous Division and extend outward through the physical being and into the tips of the thumbs, fingers, and toes.

In some cases, both the nerve and energy meridians are joined together. In many cases, however, these two types of meridians are in close proximity to one another. The ancient Chinese science of acupuncture is based on this premise.

This brings us to the next point. The tips of the thumbs and fingers are areas where healing energy can be released outward. All the ends of the thumbs and fingers contain both nerve energy and healing energy.

The palms of the hands also possess these two types of energies. It is here that the palm or hand chakras are located. The hands can be used together with the thumb tips and fingertips in special ways for healing purposes. Both the hands and their respective chakras or energy centers work in unison. Along with the healing points of the thumbs and fingers, this creates the potential for powerful healing opportunities.

A special exercise called the Hand Chakra Opening Technique was described on page 102 of *Ancient Teachings for Beginners*. Some of you may have already tried this technique and found that you were able to open up the palm chakras. Some warmth and pulsing energy felt in the hands may have been the results. For those of you who have not tried this exercise, you might consider trying this technique as described in that book.

Many of you who are spiritually awakened and involved in the healing field may already have your palm or hand chakras fairly open. This means that you are able to warm your hands up quickly and expand the palm chakras outward. This allows more natural healing energy to flow out from your hands and into a patient or client.

There is an extension exercise that can be used to open up the hand chakras even more and allow additional healing energy to enter into the hands and feet. This preliminary exercise should be used prior to working on someone.

The Fire-and-Hand-Warming Technique

Begin by doing the Heart Chakra Breathing Technique that was covered in chapter 1. After completing the breathing exercise, just let yourself relax for a few moments. Try to let your mind relax as well. Now, take both of your hands and bring them toward each other until they are about three inches apart. Either keep the hands at about waist level or place them into your lap as you do this. This can be done while you are standing or sitting, it doesn't matter. Both hands should be just slightly cupped, yet apart from each other.

Start to focus on your hands. You can leave your eyes open or shut as you do this. This is your choice. As you focus let the warmth, blood, and energy flow down your arms and into your hands. Imagine this warm energy flowing from your shoulders downward as warm water. Do this for a few seconds (see figure 5.2).

Then, move your concentration from the arms and into the hands once again. Keep all your attention on the hands, especially the palm areas. Allow your breathing to remain normal as you continue to focus all your attention on your hands. For those of you who are natural healers, you will notice your palms warming up quickly, followed by this warmth starting to spread out from your palms to the rest of the hands, including all the thumbs and fingers. There may be some of you who still cannot feel this sensation as quickly as you would like. Do not worry; the more you practice, the easier this part of the exercise becomes.

The next part of this technique is important because almost all of you will notice the results. Now, let your mind drift for a second or two. Then picture yourself outside on a warm summer night, sitting in front of a campfire. If you need to, remember a time in your life when you experienced a similar situation. This helps to bring the sensations along with the memories to the surface of your thoughts and allows you to create the desired effect.

Nerve and energy meridian endings at
thumb and fingertips

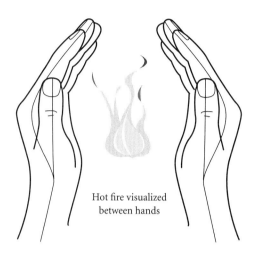

Hot fire visualized
between hands

Space (about 3 inches) between slightly cupped hands

Figure 5.2: Proper position for the Fire-and-Hand-Warming Technique.

As you are sitting before the fire, either in your imagination or through memory recall, see yourself putting your hands toward the very warm campfire. Feel the palms and the rest of the hands becoming warmer and warmer as you move them closer toward the flickering fire. In your mind, notice the various colors of the campfire as you hold your hands out. See the red, orange, blue, and white colors dancing and moving. Then, start to see and sense these colors blending together into one color only, the color white. Feel, see, or imagine this white light as a very hot white fire. As you do, allow this white fire to now exist between the palms of your hands. Concentrate all your attention on this hot, white energy as it pulses outward, barely touching your palms. Your hands may start to become sweaty, very warm and even start to pulse or tingle while doing this. Let these pulsing, tingling, or warm sensations continue for several seconds until you feel it is enough.

At that point return to normal consciousness and pull your hands away from each other. Put them down by your side. Most or all the areas of your hands will continue to feel warm for sometime after completing the Fire-and-Hand-Warming Technique.

This exercise will help if you suffer from poor circulation or your hands feel cold all the time. Increased blood circulation, nerve energy, and healing energy will be directed into the hands easier and more quickly.

Once you have finished this technique, you are now ready to do your healing work. Obviously, your clients or subjects will also receive benefits from this procedure when you perform your particular modality on them. They should notice a discernible increase in the warmth and energy associated with your hands.

This exercise will become second nature for you as you use it as part of your regimen. If you do not already have the ability to warm or "energize" your hands, you will soon develop it. Many people who are attuned to working with energy and meditating can accomplish this energizing of the hands almost immediately. Gifted healers are examples of this. This is the goal for everyone to aim toward. When you can draw this healing energy or chi into your hands and activate these energy centers, you start to bring more Universal Energy through into all of your body. This is beneficial for your own health.

It should be mentioned at this time that not everyone has warm energy residing within the hands and feet. There are some individuals who have a cooler touch or energy coming from their hands. This does not necessarily mean that these people lack healing gifts. Some people simply work with a cooler, gentle energy when they do healing work on others.

The following ancient healing methods will now be covered in detail with you. These can be used to augment your own healing modalities.

One day soon medical science and society will fully recognize the value of ancient healing systems. The mind, body, and soul must be taken into consideration. Fortunately, more and more people are starting to recognize this. Even mainstream science is starting to explore this crucial concept.

The suffering associated with cancer, arthritis, depression, and many other human disorders can be lessened or alleviated when these techniques are employed. As a human being you should use all the options at your disposal to maintain or regain your health. Both contemporary and complementary medicines should be considered when you or someone you know is in that difficult situation.

Eye-Strengthening Exercise

This particular exercise is quite easy to do and can be used for the following reasons. If your eyes are strained and sore, you can send healing energy into them in order to soothe and rejuvenate them. Optic nerves can be energized if needed. If the muscles associated with your eyes are weak and stressed, healing energy can help to revitalize them. Finally, those who have slight vision problems that are continuing to degenerate, this unique exercise can help to slow down this degeneration, which is usually associated with aging.

The benefits of the Eye-Strengthening Exercise can be temporary in most cases. However, there are certain situations when the benefits of doing this exercise can last for a long period of time. Trying this technique several times over three or four days seems to increase the positive results.

Either the Fire-and-Hand-Warming Technique just described, or the Hand Chakra Opening Technique covered in *Ancient Teachings for Beginners,* should be done first. This ensures that your hands, fingers, and thumbs are energized and ready to send healing energy.

After completing either technique, take one more deep breath in, hold it for a few seconds, and then release it. You are now ready to begin. The tips of the thumbs, index fingers, and middle fingers possess the strongest energy and nerve meridian endings. Some of you may sense a tingling or pulsing in these appendages of both hands, which indicates that a significant amount of healing and nerve energy is about to be released from the thumbs and fingertips. If you are not aware of this sensation being that strong, do not worry, you will still be able to succeed at this exercise.

Now, close both your eyes. Take your thumb, index, and middle finger of your right hand and move them up toward your right eye. Gently, but firmly place your thumb and then your two fingers over the top of the closed eyelid. If part of your eye is particularly sore or tired, move the thumb or fingers directly on top of the afflicted area. You can be lying down or sitting as you do this. Next, do the same thing with your left hand. Placing your left thumb and two fingers on top of the left eyelid. Once again, pay attention to any area of your left eye that is sore and move your thumbs or fingertips over the eye accordingly. When you have both of your hands positioned where you want them, put a very slight pressure on both eyelids with your thumbs and fingertips. Do not use too much pressure. It should be just enough for you to feel the thumbs and fingertips comfortably upon the eyes. Hold your hands in this position and take in another deep breath. After a few seconds, exhale the breath slowly through your nose or mouth.

Now, start to focus all your attention on both eyelids. Notice the warmth and slight pressure coming from your thumbs and fingertips. As you continue to do this, you will begin to feel more warmth and then a slight pulsing or tingling emanating from the tips of the appendages. Just relax and keep concentrating on your eyes. Soon, you will become aware of the tingling sensation becoming stronger. It is at this point that the tingling or pulsing sensations will start to move from the thumbs and fingers into the eyelids.

This tingling will continue flowing into the eyes and even into the optic nerves behind the eyeballs. This is the healing energy and nerve energy moving from the hands and appendages into the eyes and surrounding areas. Even the eye muscles will begin to receive this energy. The healing energy is also a form of the Universal Energy or Divine Energy, which is all around us. This energy emanates from the heavenly fields and vibrates down into our earthly realm.

Allow this flow of energy to continue for roughly five minutes. As the nerve and healing energies work into the eyes, strain, discomfort, and irritation within these areas will start to disappear. Soon your eyes will feel better. You may even feel a warm, pleasant sensation in both of your eyes. After approximately five minutes, you can stop the Eye-Strengthening Exercise, for a very simple reason. This area of your body that you have sent healing energy to has accepted as much as it can.

If you use this analogy, it will help. Think of the eyes as two empty cups. You have a container filled with water or liquid. This liquid represents both healing energy and nerve energy. As you pour the water into the cups they will soon start to fill up. As soon as the cups are completely full, you stop pouring the liquid into them. Obviously, this is because the cups cannot hold any more liquid or energy. The eyes, and for that matter any other organ or part of your body, can only absorb so much energy. Once the saturation level has been reached, no more energy will be able to flow into these areas for a while.

When performing this special eye treatment, five minutes seems to be the amount of time for this saturation level to occur. Many people may know on a conscious level when they have reached that point. Your intuitive abilities have a tendency to tell you when to stop.

As you finish this exercise, remove both hands from your eyes. Put your hands comfortably into your lap if sitting, or if you are standing, lower your hands to your sides. Take a few deep and relaxing breaths and then go about your business.

After completing the Eye-Strengthening Exercise for the first time, go to a mirror and look at your eyes. If you were successful at directing these energies into your eyes, you will notice that the eyeballs seem brighter and clearer looking. The eyes may even appear to have a sparkle emanating from them. This is an indication that the treatment worked.

Depending on the severity of the problem existing with your eyes, you can repeat this exercise when needed. If your eyes are merely sore, doing this exercise once or even a second time the next day should prove sufficient. On the other hand, if your eyes are sore and your vision seems particularly poor, trying the exercise once a day for seven consecutive days may help. After this time, you may notice that your eyesight seems stronger and the eyes feel better. Of course, always use your own discretion when you try this. Repeat the technique at a later date when you feel you need to.

There is a variation of this exercise that can be tried as well. This one can be done in place of the just mentioned Eye-Strengthening Exercise or can be alternated with it.

Universal Energy has both a positive and negative essence. Under the Law of Magnetism or the Law of Electricity, there are two different polarities, positive and negative. The universe functions under the same laws. Some of the Chinese philosophies are based upon the same premise. For instance, Yin and Yang are two essences that work together and balance everything.

The human body is no exception. Everyone has both positive and negative energy existing within their bodies. These two separate energies or essences come together as one complete energy that is referred to as Universal Energy, chi, or vital life force. This was discussed in *Ancient Teachings for Beginners* as the Law of Three or the Law of the Triangle.

In the heavenly fields and on Earth as well, these two essences are needed to manifest the Universal Energy. This energy, as stated, is everywhere—it is in the air, the trees, and the water. As human beings, we need both the male and female principles to exist. Both are necessary for the manifestation of life. This is an example of how two opposites are required for balance and creation.

For most people, the right side of the body will contain more positive energy. The left side of your body will contain more negative energy. This is true in regard to your hands as well. It is almost like a battery of a car containing both negative and positive polarities. The majority of humans have this arrangement within. About 99 percent of people have the positive energy or polarity on the right side and the negative polarity on the left side. There are a few exceptions to this rule.

This brings us to the next point. In the Eye-Strengthening Exercise you put your right hand with thumb and fingertips on top of your right eyelid. You then placed your left hand on top of your left eyelid in the very same manner. This means that your right hand containing more positive polarity sent healing and nerve energy into your right eye which is also more positive. Alternately, your left hand containing more negative energy directed healing and nerve energy into your left eye that, of course, is more negative.

Under the laws of magnetism and electricity, positive attracts negative and vice versa. Like attracts unlike. This suggests that the Universal healing energy that contains both polarities will flow well if the positive energy is allowed to flow toward the negative energy and vice versa.

Although this is true, the eye technique that you just tried will still work very effectively. The required healing and nerve energy will flow into each eye unimpeded.

However, if you try the following, you may find even greater and quicker results. This time when you perform the eye strengthening exercise, put your right hand ontop of your left eyelid, instead. Allow the thumb and fingertips to be positioned in the same way as previously explained. Then, do the same thing with your left hand, placing the thumbs and fingertips on top of the right eyelid. By using this alternative technique, you may notice the tingling or pulsing sensations in your hands and appendages working

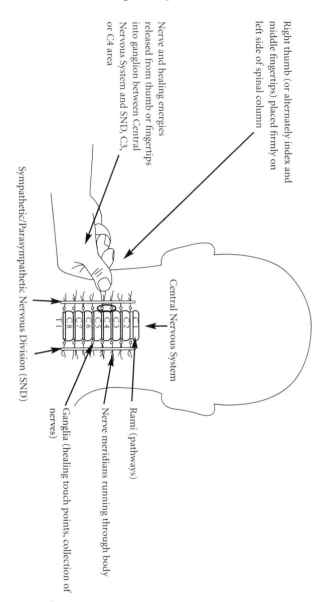

Right thumb (or alternately index and middle fingertips) placed firmly on left side of spinal column

Nerve and healing energies released from thumb or fingertips into ganglion between Central Nervous System and SND, C3, or C4 area

Sympathetic/Parasympathetic Nervous Division (SND)

Central Nervous System

Ganglia (healing touch points, collection of nerves)

Nerve meridians running through body

Rami (pathways)

T1 C8 C7 C6 C5 C4 C3 C2

Figure 5.3: Healing point and proper hand positions for Headache Removal Technique: Phase One. Note that either the right thumb, index, or middle fingers can be used.

better followed by more energy flowing into both eyes in a faster manner.

The Eye-Strengthening Exercise and the slightly altered version were given to you so that you can experiment with both ways. Try each one and then decide which works best for you. This is your choice and either way of practicing the eye exercise will work.

Headache Removal Technique: Phase One

Many of the techniques and exercises covered in this book are designed to help you become more gifted in healing. A natural progression can be made from the Fire-and-Hand-Warming Technique and the Eye-Strengthening Technique to the following exercise.

The Headache Removal Technique, phase one, is based upon the appendages of the hands being placed onto key healing touch points that exist on the human body. These healing points run along both sides of the spinal column.

If you refer back to figure 5.1, you will notice that the spinal column has four sections. These consist of the cervical (neck area), the thoracic (upper back), the lumbar (mid- to lower back), and the sacral (buttocks).

Phase one of the headache removal technique focuses on the cervical or neck area. There are eight vertebrae existing in the cervical area. These are referred to as C1 to C8. C1 being the first vertebra situated at the brain stem under the back of the skull, C8 being the last vertebra positioned at the base of the neck where the back meets.

The Central Nervous System runs directly down the middle of the spinal column including the neck. Along both sides of the Central System is the Autonomic Nervous System that consists of the Sympathetic and Parasympathetic Nervous Division, or SND for short.

Now, between the SND and the Central Nervous System are a series of ganglia that lie in a vertical row on either side of the spinal column and extend from the base of the skull to the coccyx. A single one of these is called a ganglion and it is a gathering or collection of nerves. These ganglia are special healing points existing within the body.

The Central Nervous System is connected to the SND by a series of pathways called rami. A single pathway is a ramus. These pathways extend from the central system outwards to the Sympathetic Nervous Division and Parasympathetic. Each ganglion (a collection of nerves) is situated directly in between each pathway or rami. These ganglia can be considered the center point of each pathway.

Before you attempt phase one of the headache removal technique, you should have your client or subject readied. There are two ways of doing this. Either he or she can sit down on a low back chair or lie face down on a massage or Reiki table. If using the table during this treatment, the subject's face should be positioned comfortably into the face hole. This ensures that you, as the practitioner, have unimpeded access to your client's neck area. The same holds true in regards to using a low back chair.

Next, have your client take in a few deep breaths. Two or three deep breaths should suffice. This allows the person to relax slightly and draw in some chi or universal energy into his or her body. After that, both you and your subject should take in one deep breath together. Hold it as one in unison for about three seconds and then both of you should release your breaths together slowly and evenly out the nostrils. By doing this breathing exercise together, you allow your bodies to become more attuned to each other.

Now, take your right hand that contains more positive energy and close it up into a fist. The fist should be lightly closed and not squeezed tight. Let your thumb move up away from the rest of your hand until it forms "the thumbs-up position." You are now ready to perform the headache removal technique on your subject or client.

Move your right hand to the back of the person's neck until it is just slightly above or away from the surface of the skin. Look at the neck from the base of the skull down to the lower part of the neck where it joins with the back. Use this as a reference and find the middle or midpoint of the neck. This area that you are now looking at is approximately where the C4 vertebra is located. Place your thumb gently but firmly on top of the center of the neck. Your thumb should now be touching the midpoint of the neck. You may feel a slight bump or ridge here. This is the spine of the vertebra. Carefully and slowly move your thumb up the center of the neck about one inch. You should now be directly over top of the C3 vertebra. Once again, you might feel the spine just beneath your tip of your thumb. Do not press down here. Caution should always be used when touching the spinal column, especially in the cervical area.

From this point, gently move your right thumb and hand just slightly to the left of the spine. The movement should be only a fraction of an inch. This will ensure that your thumb is removed from on top of the spine and into the area next to it. If you have done this correctly your thumb is now positioned over a ganglion and nerve pathway that exists between the central nervous system and the autonomic nervous division that consists of the sympathetic and parasympathetic nervous division (SND). Refer to Figure 5.3 if needed.

Remember the reason you moved your right hand over to the left side of your subject's spine. This is based on the Law of Magnetism that was just explained in the Eye-Strengthening Exercise. Your right hand contains more positive elements of chi or Universal Energy. The left side of your client's spine and body is more negatively oriented. This is a healing touch point. If you have moved your hand over too far to the left, you will be directly on top of left trunk of the SND. You will be able to tell this by the sense of feeling. It will feel hard, like strong muscles, directly under your thumb tip. If that is the case then simply move your right thumb back toward the spine a fraction of an inch. Do not place your thumb on top of the spine but just beside it. This is the ideal location. If you practice this a few times, you will become comfortable with finding this healing point. As well, you can learn to find the other healing points that exist up and down the spine.

Once you have your thumb tip placed over the proper healing point, hold it here. Using your thumb put some light pressure on the surface of the skin. Do not press down too heavily. You should press down enough that you can feel something beneath the surface. That is all. Continue holding your thumb in this position for about five minutes.

As you do this you may start to feel a slight pulsing under your thumb tip. This is an indication that healing and nerve energies contained within your own body are starting to combine with your client's own internal energies. This pulsing sensation may become stronger as you keep holding your thumb and hand over the healing point just beside the C3 vertebra.

Let this pulsing sensation continue. Focus on it. As a healer, you will probably start to notice that your thumb tip and fingertips are starting to pulse and tingle as well. This is a very good indication that the treatment is working.

The nerve energy and healing energy of your right hand will start to flow strongly and evenly out the thumb and into the healing touch point of your client's neck. You will even feel the tingling or pulsing sensations in the other fingers of your right hand, especially your index and middle finger. In fact, the whole hand may start to pulse like a heartbeat as you continue directing healing and nerve energy into your subject. This means that a tremendous amount of healing energy is being released through you.

This Universal Energy, which also contains the nerve energy, will begin to flow up the back of the head and into the muscles under the scalp and finally down into the forehead. As this happens, the muscles will start to relax allowing undue tension to be released and pain to ease, in most cases. During the treatment ask your subject what he or she is feeling and pay particular attention to what they tell you.

If your client is a "natural energy feeler," he or she will benefit greatly from this headache removal technique. Your subject will feel the energy flowing through very quickly and effortlessly into the intended area. On the other hand, you may occasionally work with someone who is partially 'shut down'. In this case the person will feel little or no energy coming into their body because they have not learned to experience their own chi, or life force contained within.

Do not worry about this situation. It is not your fault. Your client or subject must find a way to release their emotional and physical blocks in order to begin to feel their own body and vital life force. Regimens such as Tai Chi or Yoga are two methods that can be used to help these individuals release these blocks and open up to their divine energy within themselves and all around them.

In most cases, the first phase of the Headache Removal Technique will work for most people.

It was mentioned previously that there are healing points existing up and down the spine. Obviously, the healing touch point in the close vicinity of C3 is only one of many healing points that you can use in order to help your clients. Each area of the spine corresponds with organs, glands and tissues of the body. For instance, if a person has problems with the eyes or ears, the same approach can be used to treat them.

In this case, keep your right thumb along the left side of the neck as you move it down slightly until you are at the midpoint of the neck. Once again, this is just beside the C4 vertebra. Push down lightly and hold your thumb here for a few seconds.

Check with your client. Ask him or her what they feel. The energy may not be flowing exactly where you want it to go. Your subject may feel the energy working into the throat instead. In that situation, move your thumb either up or down very slightly. Feel free to experiment with the movement of your right thumb over these areas of the neck. Continue to ask your subject what they feel as you experiment with these different healing touch points. It may take a few attempts at first but you will eventually find the proper touch point associated with the eyes or ears.

This same approach can be used for the rest of the spinal column and body. If a client has a problem in the stomach, you would move your right hand down accordingly. You would then place the thumb onto the left side of the spine in the thoracic section. If you need to, have your client turn sideways for a minute as he or she is lying on the table. Look at the stomach area and then move your gaze from that area, across the ribs and into the back. Have him or her turn back onto their stomach with the face placed into the face hole. You should then place your right thumb onto the ganglion located directly to the left of the T6 vertebra. Your subject should be able to help you by providing feedback.

Of course, attempting this type of treatment while your subject is sitting in a low back chair is impractical. Always make sure that the person is lying face down in a comfortable position.

Keep in mind that the organs and glands of the body as viewed from the front or side, correspond with the healing touch points existing up and down the spine. If you drew a straight line from where the heart is located through into the back, then you would have the approximate place where the healing touch point is located. This guideline should give you a general idea of where to place your right thumb along the spine.

Most of you will use the tip of the right thumb as you give a treatment. However, you can also use your index and middle finger of your right hand in the same manner. In this case, just place the tips of both fingers onto the appropriate healing point or ganglion. This alternative position works as well as the thumb tip method. This is your choice. Simply use the method that is more comfortable for you.

The Role of the
Sympathetic Nervous Division

The following information will explain how the Sympathetic Nervous Division and the Central Nervous System play a major role in this ancient healing process. As described, the healing and nerve energies will work into the ganglion and out the nerve pathway and into the SND. As these energies enter into the sympathetic, they will begin to change somewhat.

The frequency or rate of vibrations associated with healing energy, chi or vital life force is extremely high. It cannot be truly measured by any scientific machines existing today. This high vibration of energy that is connected to the heavenly fields needs to be lowered to a frequency that is more "in sync" with the physical body and natural nerve energy.

As yet, medical science does not recognize the true value of the Sympathetic Nervous Division. In reality, the SND is in sympathy with the Divine Energy or Universal

Energy that surrounds us and originates from the Creator or Godsource.

One of its important functions involves the reception and assimilation of the chi or Universal Energy. This is accomplished in the following manner. Consider the field of electronics for a moment. In it there are devices called step down transformers that are responsible for lowering rates of vibrations or frequencies from one level to another. This same concept was mentioned in *Ancient Teachings for Beginners* in regard to the pineal and pituitary glands. The SND has the ability to receive this energy in its extremely high vibratory rate and lower it into a frequency or rate of vibration that is fully in harmony with the glands, organs, tissues, and cells of the human body. This energy will work together with the nerve energy.

The Divine Energy can enter into the Sympathetic system through two methods. The first involves the human auric field. The second way of course involves the touch point healing technique.

Your energy field or aura is very sensitive to all types of energies, psychic impressions, emotions, and sensations that surround you in your everyday world. It is especially sensitive to the Universal Energy. This energy can enter into your auric field and the chakras and then be absorbed into the SND. The Sympathetic is closely attuned to the human aura and chakra system. As it enters the SND, it will "step down" to a lower frequency and then be released from here and out into the nerve meridians that exist throughout the whole body. Both your client's nerve energy and your nerve energy will join together and combine with this Universal healing energy and flow outward into the body.

By working as a partnership, you and your subject will be successful in letting the treatment unfold. As stated, you should keep your right thumb on this point for about five minutes and then remove it gently once the saturation level has been reached. Then, step back approximately three feet from your subject. This ensures that you have removed yourself from his or her auric field.

Headache Removal Technique: Phase Two

The next phase of the Headache Removal Technique involves the use of both of your hands. In this case, your subject can be treated while sitting comfortably in a low back chair. Of course, you can have your client lie down on a massage table face up. However, when a person is lying down you do not have full access to all of his or her head. Nevertheless, you can still work on the head area in a limited manner.

Phase two can be used immediately following the completion of phase one of the headache removal technique. It can also be used by itself as a main treatment, if you wish. Depending on the circumstances, you may find the use of both phases more beneficial for many of your clients. In other situations, this phase of the treatment may be the best course of action to take. Use your common sense and intuition in regard to this matter.

Begin by stepping back into your subject's auric field. If your client is sitting down approach him or her from the back and place both of your warmed up hands about two inches above the head in the crown area. Then move your hands down slowly till they are positioned on each side of the head just above the ears. Remember to keep both hands away from the surface of the head. If your client is lying down, step up to the top of the massage table where the head is resting and place your hands just above the head in the same way and then move them to each side of the head gently. Take in a deep breath and hold it for about three seconds. Then release your breath through your nose evenly and return to normal breathing. Keep your hands in this position for a few moments. As you do this, start to focus on the palms of both hands. You may start to feel warmth, coolness or even a prickly sensation on the palms. This is normal and expected.

Techniques were discussed in regards to sending healing and nerve energies from both hands. As an initiated and spiritually awakened person, you are well aware that the human hands can send and receive energy, as well. Many adept healers will send or direct energy from one hand, and at the same time, receive or draw energy into the other hand. Most will use the right hand to send out energy, while the left hand acts as a receiver. However, some healers will do this in a reverse fashion, using the left hand to send or direct energy and letting the right accept energy. Either method is fine. There is no right or wrong way of doing this.

It should be mentioned and understood at this time that the receiving hand can draw in or receive energy that is not of a healing nature. Although this hand has the potential to receive healing energy, in most cases, it will be used to draw in negative, unhealthy energy or vibrations.

As you start to feel sensations on both of your palms, let yourself focus on one of your hands. For the sake of simplicity, the right hand will be used as the example. Continue to concentrate on your right hand, letting the healing or Universal Energy flow through the palms, thumbs, and fingers. Even though your hands are positioned slightly away from the surface of the head, this energy will work its way into the designated area near your right hand.

You should check with your client as to where the pain is located as you do this. This perception check should be done periodically through the remainder of the treatment. Use your discretion.

As you send energy with your right hand, shift some of your attention to the other hand. Imagine yourself pulling in negative energy and other sensations into the left hand. Think of it as a magnet or vacuum drawing all the pain from your client's headache directly into the thumb, fingers and the whole hand itself. Of course, negative energy in this case refers to unhealthy vibrations as compared to the negative element in electronics. Soon, you will start to experience prickly sensations or even some type of strange warmth moving into the hand. In rare situations, you might even feel a cool energy. Let this negative energy consisting of pain, anger, and tension continue moving slowly past the wrist and into the forearm. Feel this sensation working into the arm.

Now, focus once more on your right hand or sending hand. Notice the hand pulsing as universal healing energy, along with some nerve energy, flows out the palms, finger-tips, and thumb. Let yourself direct this special energy toward the afflicted area of your subject's head. As you practice this, the healing energy will actually flow straight to its intended area. When this happens, more of the unhealthy energy or vibration will be pushed toward the receiving hand.

At this point, you will feel the prickly or uncomfortable sensations moving up the arm until they reach the elbow. Once the negative energy has reached this juncture, it is important that you remove your left hand or receiving hand from the subject's auric field. Then, remove your right hand from the aura, as well. Step back from the subject about three to four feet until you are outside of the person's energy field.

Once you have done this, shake off both of your hands, especially your left or receiving hand. If you can imagine yourself shaking water from your hands, then you will know the proper way. After this, take your right hand and brush off any residual negative energy from the left arm and hand. Repeat a second time for good measure. Then, let your left hand do the same brushing technique to your right arm.

Take in one deep breath and hold it for a few seconds and then step back into your client's energy field. Place your hands in approximately the same position and then move your right hand or receiving hand closer toward the original afflicted area.

As you do this, the area where the pain is located will become smaller and start to move toward the left hand or receiving hand. Allow this hand to move closer to the pain area until it is a few inches away. Both of your hands should now be in closer proximity to each other and located around the area where the negative energy or pain is situated.

Originally, when you started to treat your client, he or she may have experienced a great deal of discomfort. For example, the pain could have been located across the forehead. After a few moments, this afflicted area should have become smaller and moved toward the left side of the forehead, closer to the left hand, the receiving hand. Of course, if you used your hands in the reverse order, the process would occur in the opposite direction, accordingly.

Allow the healing energy to flow from your right hand into the afflicted area that is smaller and more localized. Sense the energy moving into the head. Listen to your intuition as you continue to do this. You may feel the urge to move or shift either your right or left hand above or around the area of pain. Perhaps, you will see in your own mind where both hands should be placed. Pay attention to your intuition. Allow it to guide you in this respect. You may find yourself shifting one or both hands a few times. This is normal.

As before, focus some of your attention on your left hand and feel the prickly heat or negative energy flowing into the hand much the same as a vacuum cleaner sucking in dirt. Let it move up the hand and forearm until it reaches the elbow.

Once again, remove your left hand or receiving hand from your subject and then your right hand. Step back from the aura and repeat the shaking and brushing techniques just described. Remember afterwards to take in a deep breath and hold it for a few seconds. Then, step back into the client's aura around the crown chakra and continue with the Headache Removal Technique.

You may find that you have to repeat this procedure several times depending on the situation. If your subject is very receptive to any type of energy work, including Reiki, he or she will probably allow the pain and negative vibrations to be removed from the head and aura very quickly. This is done either on a conscious or subconscious level by the person. In this case, you may only have to perform this procedure two or three times. However, if your client is not as receptive to energy healing, you might have to do this several times. Also, the person's level of pain may influence this. In any event, proceed with the treatment. Use your intuition in regard to all of this.

Eventually, the amount of pain or negative, unhealthy energy that your left hand or receiving hand draws in will lessen. Soon you will feel few or no prickly sensations and negativity in your thumb, fingers, and palm of this hand. This is an indication that the treatment is complete.

Normally, the Headache Removal Technique takes any where from ten minutes to forty-five minutes. If you were to continue this special headache removal treatment any longer than the maximum amount of time suggested, there would be little result. The reason for this is simple.

It was mentioned earlier in the Eye-Strengthening Technique section about the saturation level of healing energy. Once a part of the human body receives a certain amount of universal or divine energy, it becomes full or saturated and cannot receive any more. Remember the analogy of the empty cup being filled. This is the same idea.

Sometimes, if the individual you are working on is very sensitive to energy, they will be aware of this, as well. The healing energy that flowed from your right hand or sending hand will lessen. Think of a tap fully open allowing the water to pour forth. Slowly, the water flow lessens as the tap is gradually turned off. The Divine Intelligence of the Universe is involved in all of this. Also, your client's higher self influences this healing process.

Once you have finished the treatment, step away from your subject's auric field for a final time. Do not forget to shake off your hands and follow with the brushing method described. Allow your client to sit or lie there a few minutes until he or she is ready to get up.

Immediately after your subject has left wash your hands thoroughly with warm water and soap. Make sure that you wash up to your elbows.

There is final thing to do. Either while sitting or standing focus on both of your forearms and hands. Imagine or feel yourself sending white light and healing energy down the forearms and out the hands. Allow any residual negative vibrations that may be contained within the aura in the vicinity of your hands to be removed using white light. Feel and sense this white light expanding outward from your hands and forearms. Now, draw in one more deep breath and hold for about three seconds. Then release your breath slowly and return to normal breathing.

If you work as a healer, counselor or teacher, it is important that you follow the clearing and cleansing procedures just mentioned. The Headache Removal Technique is one method of deliberately pulling in or drawing negative energy into your aura. Inadvertently, you can pull in negative vibrations and "bad energy" from others as well.

If this type of unhealthy energy gets absorbed too far into your auric field and remains there for too long, it will work its way through the chakras, into the nervous system and eventually into your body. The result may be a cold, flu symptoms, or a general feeling of tiredness. That is why you should not let the prickly sensations, heat, or unpleasant sensations move past the elbow when doing the headache removal technique.

Generally speaking, you might also experience uncomfortable emotions such as anger, worry, or fear. In this case, you have picked up the negative emotions from some of your clients. Some of you may be feeling these conditions on a regular basis. If so, then you need to start practicing these clearing and cleansing methods regularly.

The Headache Removal Technique can be expanded and used for any part of the body. For instance, if someone is suffering from lower back pain, your hands can be used in a similar fashion.

As an initiated and spiritually awakened healer or counselor, you are empathic and sensitive to other people and to their auric fields. You are also well aware of the higher vibrations or Universal Energy that exists all around you. This allows you to work in this world and still maintain a spiritual connection to the angels and heavenly fields above.

> "You can sense energy to the degree your heart is open and loving . . ."
>
> —Sanaya Roman

Chapter 6

Advanced Energy Healing Techniques: Part One

"The most beautiful experience we can have is the mysterious. It is the fundamental emotion that stands at the cradle of true art and true science."

—Albert Einstein

In this chapter, advanced energy healing techniques that deal with Universal Energy, your own natural healing energy, and the human chakra system will be covered in detail.

By following these special techniques, you will enhance many of your developed abilities. You can also incorporate all of this into your own healing modalities.

Third Eye Chakra Opening Technique

This particular exercise is designed to help you open up your third eye chakra easily and quickly. As a spiritually awakened individual you are familiar with chakras and are adept at working with your own chakras or energy centers.

Begin by taking in a deep breath, hold it for five seconds and then release it slowly. Next, take your index and middle finger of one hand and touch your forehead with the fingertips. Use a slight pressure as you do so. If you are right handed, use your right hand and vice versa. Keep your fingertips there for a few brief seconds and then remove them putting your hand back down into your lap or by your side.

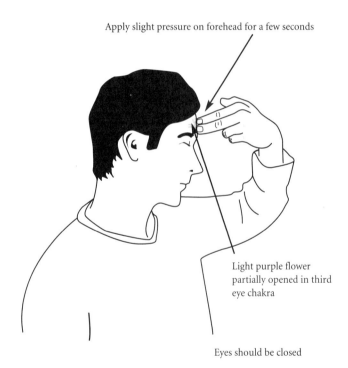

Apply slight pressure on forehead for a few seconds

Light purple flower partially opened in third eye chakra

Eyes should be closed

Figure 6.1: Placement of fingertips for the Third Eye Chakra Opening Technique

As you do this, start to focus on your forehead or third eye. Still feel or imagine the slight pressure of your fingers in this spot. This pressure should be about two inches in diameter. Let this sensation spread across the third eye area until it is roughly twice this size.

Now take your attention inward and allow this pressure or sensation to move below the surface of the forehead about an inch. Feel this sensation getting stronger just beneath the skin in the third eye. Concentrate on this area an inch below the forehead until you sense a gentle pulsing or warmth here. At this point, you will use a variation of the Flower Opening Technique that was described in *Ancient Teachings for Beginners.*

Allow yourself to visualize or imagine a beautiful light purple flower all closed up in this area of your third eye. In your mind, see and sense the petals of this flower slowly opening up in the same manner that a flower opens to the warmth of the sun's rays.

Feel and see these petals unfolding even more across the third eye. Enjoy the warmth of the sun spreading across the forehead as these flower petals open up. Then, start to think of warm, soothing water beginning to flow across the skin of the forehead and even beneath the surface. Feel this warm water as it expands outward through the third eye and at the same time visualize the light purple flower petals expanding also. Continue doing this until the flower has fully opened across the forehead from temple to temple. Let the warmth of the sun and water flow across here.

Now just enjoy the warm feelings for a few moments. You may even feel a pulsing or tingling sensation spreading across the forehead and deep into the front of the head. This is an indication that the pineal gland within the lower part of the brain is being affected. The gland starts to vibrate slightly and becomes activated. As mentioned before, the pineal, once activated, will affect the third eye chakra in turn. This energy center will become activated and open up. This allows your intuitive and creative abilities to open up quickly and even increase significantly.

Try practicing the Third Eye Opening Technique a few times until you become proficient at it. Some of you will feel and notice some tangible results the first time that you experiment with this exercise. This is due to the fact that you are very sensitive to energy. For most of you, it will take a few attempts until you get the most results. After this it will become second nature for you to open your third eye in a quick and profound manner.

There will be a few of you who will have to practice this technique several times until some results are obtained. This occurs when you are slightly blocked and not as sensitive to your body and the natural energy. A "block" exists when you have emotional or physical problems that prevent you from allowing the energy to flow into and through your body. This can happen on either a conscious or subconscious level. Being aware of this is the first step to removing a block. By practicing this technique some of the blocks will dissolve. In a short period of time, you will succeed and experience positive results. Soon, it will become easier for you to open up your third eye chakra quickly.

Along with enhancing your intuitive and creative abilities there are other benefits to performing the Third Eye Opening Technique.

For instance, you may start to see and sense the human energy field around others in greater detail. This may include the ability to see colors around people and not just the white light close to the body. If you can already see and sense these colors, there is a possibility that you will see them more vividly. In some cases, you may also experience past-life recall while in a relaxed state. If you already experience this phenomena, there is a chance that you will experience even more and in greater clarity.

Many of you, may start to see and sense healing energy or Universal Energy at a stronger level. You will be able to sense and know where the blocks are in someone and direct healing energy in a more proficient manner. After completing the Third Eye Opening Technique successfully you can then move onto the next important exercise.

White Grape Exercise

This particular exercise is designed to greatly affect the pituitary gland. It will also affect the pineal gland somewhat. When this happens, the pituitary will become activated and in turn influence the crown chakra. This allows the crown to awaken and open up. The already opened third eye chakra will expand even more.

Begin by shutting your eyes and draw in a deep breath. Hold it for a few seconds and then exhale slowly. Return to normal breathing. Now, focus on your third eye again. This time feel a pressure, tingling, or other sensation going deeper inside. Feel or imagine the warmth of the sun penetrating through the forehead and into the head. At the same time, sense or envision warm water flowing inside, as well.

Let the warmth of the sun and water continue penetrating until the sensations are felt directly in the middle of the head. This area is the base of the brain where both the pituitary and pineal glands are located. Concentrate on this point right in the middle of your head. The warmth or sensations may start to get stronger as you do so.

Then picture a small white grape about the size of a pea positioned here. Visualize or sense this white grape starting to vibrate slowly back and forth within. As you focus on it, feel it vibrating faster and faster. Imagine or see this grape moving rapidly back and forth. Let yourself see, feel or sense this for a few moments. Enjoy the sensations.

Now, imagine a white light within the grape. See or sense it starting to pulse inside the grape. Allow the pulsing light to expand outward from the grape until it encompasses all of it. Let this pulsing get stronger and stronger.

At this point, a variation of the Crown Chant mentioned in chapter 3 will be attempted. Feel free to review this if needed.

As before, take in a deep breath. Hold it for about three seconds. This time chant M-A-A-A-Y-Y-Y until all your breath has been released. Remember to tone this special sound in a mid range, not too high and not too low. Let yourself direct this sound or vibration into the area of the head that you are focusing on. Repeat this chant again in the same way. Direct the tone into the middle of the head, again. Even let the vibration work through the rest of your head.

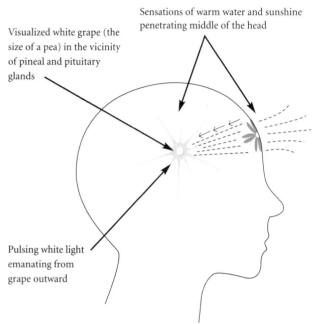

Visualized white grape (the size of a pea) in the vicinity of pineal and pituitary glands

Sensations of warm water and sunshine penetrating middle of the head

Pulsing white light emanating from grape outward

Fully opened light purple flower (indicates opened third eye chakra)

Figure 6.2: Approximate location of the white grape for the White Grape Exercise.

Relax for a moment and return to normal breathing. Maintain your attention on the white grape and the surrounding area. As you do this, you may notice that you feel lightheaded or spacey. Physiologically, you may feel warmth or tingling sensations within the middle of your head and upwards into the brain. These same sensations may be felt in the third eye chakra as well. These are indications that the pituitary gland, near the lower part of the brain, has vibrated or resonated with the sound of the MAY chant. This has activated the pituitary, balanced it, and affected the hypothalamus part of the brain. As stated earlier in chapter 2, endorphins and other secretions are being released into the body. This in turn starts to awaken, activate, and open up the crown chakra. When this happens, your crown energy center is able to tune into higher vibrations from above.

Of course, the pineal gland vibrates also and activates itself even more. This allows certain physiological and biological events to occur. The third eye energy center will open up even further as a result of this. Refer to the Final Initiation chart in chapter 2 regarding this chakra and the crown chakra.

Each person is different and will be affected in different ways when attempting this exercise. If you are a natural energy feeler, you may experience a great deal of sensations and energy throughout all of the head and even into the body, as well. You may feel very relaxed. Many of you, when you initially try this, may sense pressure or some sensation of warmth or tingling in the middle of the head and perhaps into other parts of your head, including the forehead and back of the head. This is a good sign that the exercise is working.

Some of you may feel very little when you first attempt the White Grape Exercise. Do not be discouraged. The more you practice this technique, the more success you will have. Persistence is the key in this situation. Eventually, you will receive the same results as a person who is a natural energy feeler. After completing the White Grape Exercise, you can move onto the next exercise, which is closely connected.

The Crown Chakra
Opening and Clearing Technique

This special technique is a continuation of the previous exercise. It can also be tried on its own once you are adept at performing these techniques.

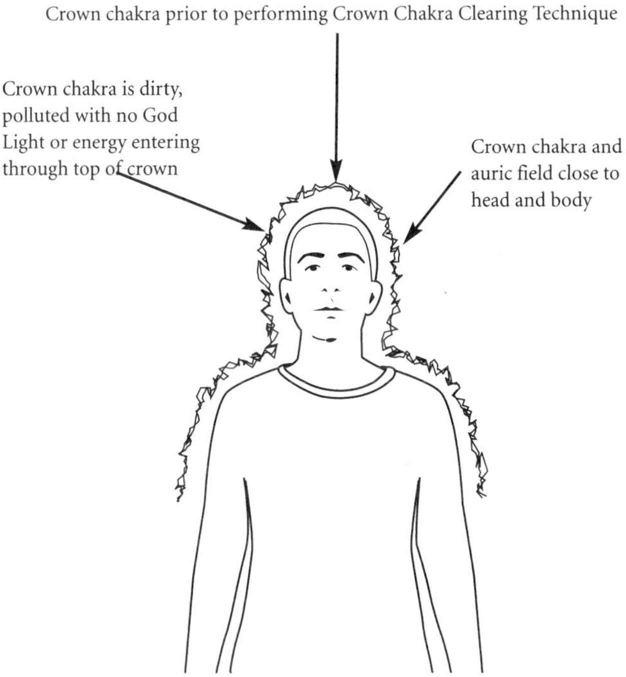

Crown chakra prior to performing Crown Chakra Clearing Technique

Crown chakra is dirty, polluted with no God Light or energy entering through top of crown

Crown chakra and auric field close to head and body

Figure 6.3: Crown chakra of a person not connected to the Creator or Godsource.

Relax for a few moments and focus on your breathing as you do so. Allow yourself to feel the sensations associated with the last exercise. Enjoy the warmth, tingling or any other sensations. Now, return all your attention to the middle of your head where the imaginary white grape is located. Concentrate on that area for about two or three seconds.

Then, feel the warmth and white light there beginning to move upward through the brain. Feel or sense this energy as warm water and sunshine as it moves from the white grape. Let this sensation continue to flow upward through the brain until it reaches the top of the head where the crown chakra is situated. You can also visualize in your head this energy as it flows from the white grape upward into the crown energy center.

When you reach this center, take in one more deep breath and hold it for about five seconds and then release it slowly. After doing this, take your right or left hand and move it to the top of your head in the crown chakra area. Touch the top of your head with two fingers, lightly. Use your index and middle finger when you touch the head. After that, put your hand down beside you or in your lap.

Start to concentrate on the top of your head where your two fingers just touched. Notice the slight pressure or sensation here. Imagine that the fingers are still pressing down upon the scalp. Focus on this for a few moments.

Now, it is time to repeat the MAY chant again. This time as you draw in a deep breath and tone M-A-A-A-Y-Y-Y, concentrate all your attention on the crown chakra. As you release all your breath while chanting this sound feel the vibration working into the crown chakra. Direct the chant into the top of your head. You may start to notice a tingling sensation in this area of your head. You may even feel light-headed as you do this chant.

Relax for a few moments. Then repeat the MAY chant in the same way. Let the vibration of sound work through the top of the head and even into the middle of the head. Keep all your attention on the crown as you tone this special chant.

The sensation of tingles upon the top of your head may increase after completing the MAY chant for a second and final time. Perhaps a slight warmth or pressure may also be experienced here. This indicates that the crown energy center is opening up more.

Once you have completed this part of the Crown Opening technique, you are now ready to continue with the next step.

Allow yourself to rest for a few minutes as you experience the results of the toning or chanting. Feel the energy or tingling sensations upon the head. Enjoy the sensations as they continue. You might even feel the tingling energy or warmth spreading completely over all of the head. Allow it to work through the scalp, hair, and down the front and back of the head. Just experience this for a moment or two.

Now, with your eyes shut, visualize or imagine a beautiful white rose all closed up on the top of your head. This white rose is a representation of the crown chakra. Still allow yourself to feel the energy or sensations on the top of the head. As you do this, imagine that you are outside on a warm summer day. Feel the sun's warmth penetrating through the top of the head about an inch below the surface of the scalp. Just imagine that you are sitting there on the beach or side of a hill enjoying the rays of the sun as they continue to pour through the top of the head where the crown chakra is situated.

As you do this, visualize the white rose starting to open up. See and sense the white flower petals unfolding as the sunrays shine onto the rose. Feel the warmth here as the petals unfold even further. Sense or picture the petals spreading across the top of the head and inside the head just below the surface. In your mind, picture and feel the flower petals becoming fully opened and expanded across the top of the head, through the top part of your brain and even down the sides and back of the head. Let the flower petals expand until they are enveloping the entire crown energy center. Sense the warmth or sensations completely throughout the top part of your head.

Let this sensation or warmth become stronger. Then, imagine warm water starting to spread through the crown chakra and opened flower petals. Let this warm, soothing water flow over the scalp, down both sides of the head, and the back of the head. Even feel or imagine this warm water flowing down into the third eye area just above the eyebrows. Focus on this for a few seconds. Enjoy the sensations of warmth or tingling energy.

Now the MAY chant should be repeated one final time. As before, take in a deep breath, hold it for a moment and then chant M-M-A-A-Y-Y-Y slowly out your mouth until all your breath has been expelled. Focus on the crown chakra area, directing the vibration of the chant here. Let the sound work through the top of the head and into the brain itself.

After toning MAY return to normal breathing. Let yourself relax but continue to concentrate on the crown chakra for several moments. Notice the sensations such as warmth or tingling on the crown energy center and all of the head, including the face in some cases. These physiological effects are normal and indicate that both the crown and third eye chakras are both fully open and activated. You can refer to the Final Initiation chart in chapter three for details.

It is at this point that you are now able to channel information, knowledge and healing energy from a higher source. This includes communicating and working safely with your angels and spirit guides.

This technique also helps to clear negative colors from your auric field, allowing it to expand and become brighter and cleaner looking.

Channeling Divine Energy or Universal Energy

Many of you may find that you are able to channel Divine Energy or Universal Energy through your crown and into your chakras and body after completing The Crown Chakra Opening and Clearing Technique. This can be accomplished by simply asking for energy to come down through the top of your head. Feel the healing energy or Divine Energy entering into the crown chakra about twelve inches above the head. Let this high vibration of energy work down through the scalp and into the body. Direct or visualize this wonderful healing energy flowing right through the body from the top of the head. Experience it as warm water flowing through you and out your feet. Let this energy flow through your whole being for a few minutes. Then slow the flow down and finally stop it completely.

Return to normal consciousness. Look around your environment in order to bring the mind back to a more normal state of awareness.

Some of you who are natural energy feelers may experience this energy flow through the body without making a conscious effort to do so. If this occurs, do not worry. Just allow the energy to flow through you and out your feet. This should be considered as a gift from God or the Creator. It allows tremendous amounts of healing energy to work into your aura, chakras, body and internal organs.

For most of you, though, you will have to ask for the energy to flow into you and direct it with a concerted effort. This may take some time but eventually, you will become quite adept at bringing Universal Energy into your whole being.

Once you have finished this, take in one deep breath, hold it for a few seconds. Release it and then return to normal breathing. Go back to your regular business, feeling refreshed and invigorated.

Warm Shower Technique

The following technique can be used to further cleanse your aura and chakras. There are other ramifications associated with this special exercise and the previous one.

The Crown Chakra Opening and Clearing Technique along with the Warm Shower Technique allows you to get in touch with the Creator and Divine or God Energy from above. Negative energy consisting of dirty, polluted colors within the aura and chakras are removed from your auric field. When this happens, negative and unwanted spirits move away from you and your energy field at the same time. This also allows angels, spirit guides and other heavenly helpers to come around you. When your aura and chakras become cleaner and brighter, you raise the vibrations of your body, soul and aura. This higher vibration attracts these beings of light and spirit guides to you and makes it much easier for them to work and communicate with you.

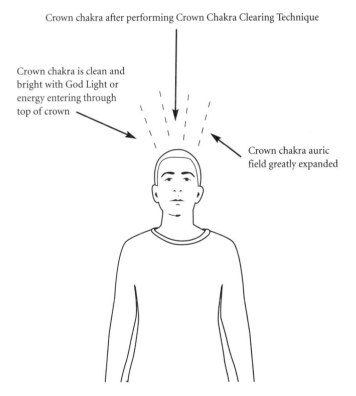

Crown chakra after performing Crown Chakra Clearing Technique

Crown chakra is clean and bright with God Light or energy entering through top of crown

Crown chakra auric field greatly expanded

Figure 6.4: Crown chakra of a person directly connected to the Creator or Godsource.

This exercise can be done once you have completed the Crown Chakra Opening and Clearing Technique. The Warm Shower Technique can also be done by itself anytime you wish.

Begin by focusing on the top of your head once more. Keep your eyes closed as you do so. Take in another deep breath and hold it for a few seconds. Then release it slowly and evenly through your nose. Return to regular breathing.

Now, imagine that you are taking a very warm shower. Feel the warm water cascading down onto your crown chakra and the top of your head. Allow this soothing warm water to flow over the top of the head, across the scalp and down the front, back, and both sides of your head. Let this warm energy pour down the back of the head, neck and into the upper shoulders. At the same time feel this soothing warmth moving down the face, over the throat area and into the upper chest.

Continue to sense the warm water flowing down from above. As you do, let the flow of water or warmth become stronger until it pours down over the head and into the upper back and upper chest. Focus on this energy and continue to move it down over both the front and back of your body at the same time. Concentrate on this shower of water flowing down through the heart chakra, over the breasts and down into the solar plexus just above the navel. Feel this wonderful water spreading across the solar energy center and stomach area. Let the warm healing water move across the skin until it has spread completely across this part of the body. Then let it move down past the belly button, into the sacral plexus and across the surface of the skin until it has spread from hip to hip. Continue to experience this shower of warm water flowing down into the base chakra and thighs. Enjoy this warm energy.

If you need to, think back to when you took a shower recently and recall the warm and soothing sensations of warm water flowing and cascading over the skin and all over the body as it moved downward. Direct the flow of warm water or energy down the thighs, over the knees, ankles, and feet. Feel the flow of warm sensations moving across the toes and out the bottoms of your feet.

Now, move your focus from your feet back up into the shoulders and upper back. Imagine and feel the wonderful and warm water flowing down rapidly over the middle and lower back, and into the buttocks. Even feel this energy or pleasant sensation moving down the spinal column, as well. From here, allow the energy to flow quickly down the back of the legs and out the bottoms of the heels.

Then, from the top of the head let the warm water flow down completely over the body and out the bottoms of your feet. Allow this soothing and healing energy to envelope your body and energy field.

Experience this warm shower for a minute or two. Enjoy the sensations throughout all or part of the body. Sense and see the aura and body become cleaner and brighter. Even picture the energy meridians that run down the sides of your arms and legs becoming cleaner, too. When you feel that the minute or two are up, start to imagine the water beginning to slow down. Feel the energy slowing down even more. Then, move all your attention to above the top of the head at the outer perimeter of the crown chakra. Sense or see the water or energy as being completely stopped or "turned off." Return to normal consciousness and notice your surroundings. When you are ready, go back to your everyday activities.

If you have the opportunity, take a few moments to look at yourself in a mirror. The mirror should be large enough for you to see your face, head and chest area. Of course, if you are looking into a full size mirror you will be able to see all of your body. However, either size will do.

First, look at your face and then your eyes. You may notice that your face and skin look smoother and healthier when you gaze at your eyes, they may appear brighter with more of a light or twinkle within.

Be aware that this is not your imagination. You are actually seeing or sensing the results of having the higher vibrations of energy enter into your auric field, your body and ultimately your cells and organs.

After looking at your face and eyes, gaze above and around your head. You will probably notice that the crown chakra and aura appears much brighter and expanded. This indicates that you have cleansed this energy center along with this area of the aura. The third eye is also affected greatly by this and the forehead will appear cleaner. After this, gaze at the chest and heart chakra. Many of you will observe that this area looks and feels somewhat lighter and cleaner.

These are the most important areas to gaze at in order to notice or sense any positive differences. Most of you will be aware of a significant change after you have completed this special technique and the previous ones, compared to before you began.

Initially, a few of you may feel, sense, or see very little difference or perhaps nothing at all. This is nothing to be concerned over. With practice, you will develop the ability to see, sense and feel these wonderful changes as the Universal Energy and higher vibrations work through you.

If you have a full size mirror, you can continue gazing further, if you wish. If so, let yourself look at the solar plexus chakra, stomach, and along both sides of the body in this region. Then, allow your gaze to move downward in order to gaze at the area of the sacral chakra as well as along both hips. From there, gaze at the base chakra and then look along both sides of the thighs. Let your eyes move down the legs, knees and eventually into the feet. If you are very sensitive to energy and can see auras well, you may notice some white light or cleaner energy through and around these parts of the body, from the solar energy center down to the toes.

Refer to the two illustrations that show the crown chakra prior to clearing and after clearing for examples of how the crown and aura are affected by these techniques.

The Third Eye Chakra Opening Technique, the White Grape Exercise, the Crown Chakra Opening and Clearing Technique, and the Warm Shower Technique can all be done together as a progression or complete process. Each and every technique and exercise can also be attempted separately.

Once you become familiar with all of them, feel free to experiment with any or all of these special exercises. Soon, it will be second nature for you to open these chakras, clear them and work with higher vibrations of healing energy or Universal Energy. Every time you allow this energy from above into your aura, chakras, and body, you develop the ability to channel higher amounts of it. This allows your whole being to become lighter and to raise your vibrations.

After you have tried these exercises for a bit and feel comfortable with all of them, you can move to the next step. This involves applying these newly acquired techniques on your clients, patients or subjects. Use your own inner guidance to decide when you are ready to do this.

Prior to working with your clients, a few things should be explained.

Benefits of These Five Special Techniques

There are numerous benefits that can result from using any, some or all of the previously mentioned techniques. The following list covers many of these benefits.

- Stress Reduction. The use of Universal Energy and internal healing energy reduces anxiety and stress within the mind and body. Certain chemical secretions are released into the bloodstream to soothe emotions. The area of the brain associated with pleasure, the hypothalamus, is affected greatly thereby creating feelings of peace and comfort within.

- Negative Entity or Spirit Release. The positive energy associated with the Crown Chakra Opening and Clearing Technique as well as the other techniques allows the auric field and chakras to become brighter and cleaner, thereby drawing spirit guides and angels around you. This higher vibration of energy forces negative entities or spirits out of the aura and away from the person.

· Promotes Healing of Body, Mind, and Soul. The Universal energy or healing energy that flows through the aura, the chakras and the body promotes healing on all levels, body, mind and soul. This allows the person to feel balanced physically, emotionally, and spiritually.

· Acceleration of Spiritual Growth. A spiritually awakened person will develop even more spiritual insight and spirituality in a rapid and profound manner as the higher vibrations of energy work into the body, the brain, and the chakras. This allows the potential for true spiritual enlightenment to unfold.

· Acceleration of Psychic Development. A psychically awakened person will increase the psychic abilities very quickly by practicing any or all the five special techniques. Special gifts will become enhanced as other areas of the brain are awakened.

· Dramatic Slowing Down of Aging Process. Universal Energy or Divine Energy from above flows through the body and chakras. It triggers the release of kundalini or serpent power into the body via the sympathetic nervous division. This affects the hormonal secretions of the endocrine glandular system in such a way as to balance the glands and slow down the aging process greatly. The high vibration of energy also changes and revitalizes all the cells, tissues, and organs of the body. In essence the physical body becomes more of a light body.

- Increase of IQ Level. Universal Energy or Divine Energy from above enters the brain. This activates parts of the brain by the firing of neurons. These activated neurons send electrical stimulation to areas of the brain that are dormant. This awakens these areas and allows you to use more of your brain capacity.

- Greater Expansion and Cleansing of the Human Aura. The flow of Universal energy combined with the powerful energy of the chakras, including kundalini, will expand and cleanse the aura in greater amounts. The human aura will become much larger and brighter.

- More Balanced and Opened Chakras. The Universal energy and internal healing energy will balance the chakras to a greater level and allow these energy centers to become more opened and larger. This allows more Divine light or higher vibrations of energy to enter into the aura, chakras, and body.

Once you feel that you are ready, you can use any or all of these techniques to help your clients and friends. Begin by having your subject or client sit in a comfortable chair in front of you. The person should be about five feet away from you. Make sure that there is a wall directly behind the individual. A white or light-colored wall is preferable but most colors will do.

Ask your client to take in a deep breath and hold it for about five seconds. Then have her release the breath slowly out the nose or mouth. Let her return to normal breathing.

As the person begins breathing normally again, move your eyes above her head and glance at the aura in the crown chakra area. Some of you will begin to notice a slight light surrounding the head. This will appear as white and will extend a few inches outward from the head. For those of you who see auras easily, some colors along with the white light will be seen. The aura in the crown chakra area will appear even more expanded to you. Many of you may see the white light along with a subtle hint of another color such as light blue within the aura around the head. This indicates that you are developing the ability to see the human energy field or aura easier.

It does not matter if you see all the colors, a few colors, or only a slight light around the person's head as you gaze at the aura. All that is important is that you see something. This means that you have slowed down your brain wave patterns and entered into a light altered state.

Return your attention to the client's face. Have her close the eyes. Once that is done, lean or step forward and place your index and middle finger of one hand onto the person's forehead in the third eye area. Touch lightly and hold the two fingers there for about two or three seconds. Then pull your hand away and step back. If you were sitting originally, return to a sitting position.

You can perform any or all of the techniques on your clients or subjects while either standing or sitting. However, being in a sitting position during most of the time can be more comfortable for you.

Ask your friend or subject to focus on the third eye area where your fingers had just touched. Let the person feel or sense the slight pressure here in the third eye chakra area. It is at this point that you will guide your subject through the exercises and techniques. Some of you may not feel comfortable with guiding someone through these techniques at first. If so, find a close friend or relative to practice on until you build up a bit of confidence. After a few attempts you should be ready to try these special exercises on your clients or patients on a regular basis.

Most of you in a particular healing modality will be quite confident and be able to incorporate any or all of these techniques into your practice.

Now, guide your client through the Third Eye Chakra Opening Technique. Let the person continue to feel a slight sensation in the brow. Tell her to sense or imagine the pressure starting to spread until it feels about twice the circumference. As the person does this, let her also imagine or feel both warm water and sunlight spreading across the forehead just above the eyebrows. Make sure that the client focuses on this area for a few moments.

You can incorporate the Flower Opening Technique into this part of the exercise at this time. As the client concentrates on the sensations spreading across the forehead, let her see or sense a beautiful purple flower unfolding, too. The flower petals should spread completely across the forehead from temple to temple along with the flow of warm water and sunshine.

Let your client focus on this for a few more seconds and then do a perception check. Find out what sensations, if any, your subject feels. Make sure that the eyes remain shut during all of this. You have now completed the Third Eye Opening Technique on your patient, client, or friend.

Now, in one easy fluid motion you can begin the White Grape Exercise. Have your subject start to sense or feel warm energy penetrating inside about three inches. Once again, this should be pictured or felt as warm water and sunshine flowing inward until the energy is directly within the middle of the head, just at the base of the brain. At the same time, let your subject feel or sense your two fingers penetrating within along with the water and sunshine. At this point your client or patient should be focused on this area within the head. Allow the individual to continue concentrating here for a few moments.

After this, let the client visualize or imagine a little white grape situated inside the middle of the head at the base of the brain. For simplicity's sake, it is the exact center of the head that should be focused upon. Remember that the grape should be about the size of a small pea.

Incidentally, the reason for using a small white grape as a focus tool is simple. This small grape represents the pineal and pituitary glands located within this general area of the head in the lower part of the brain. When you or your client focuses on a white grape, it can help to activate either or both of these special glands within. This is one more way of opening more of your abilities or your subject's abilities.

Speak softly and slowly as you guide your subject through this. Do not worry about making mistakes. Talk quietly to the person the same way you would with an old friend. Relax and let things flow.

You are now ready to perform the MAY chant. This time, the chant or sound will be directed toward your client instead of yourself. Make sure that the person in front of you keeps the eyes shut as you do this.

Take in a deep breath and hold it for a few seconds. As you release your breath out your mouth chant M-M-M-A-A-A-Y-Y-Y. Your voice should be louder than a normal speaking level. It is similar to singing. Concentrate on your client before you as you release this powerful sound. Let yourself direct the chant toward the person's head as you expel all of your breath.

Look first at the client's third eye area as you perform this tone. Then glance above and around the head. You may start to notice or sense that the auric field around this person is changing, becoming brighter and cleaner. This is not your imagination. Your intuitive abilities are either sensing or seeing a positive change resulting from this special chant.

You should do another perception check with your client after you have directed the MAY chant toward her. Ask your client if she feels anything. Pay attention to what feedback you receive. Most people, if opened or attuned to energy, will feel some sensations such as warmth or tingling in the middle of the head or in the forehead. A few will feel it throughout the entire head including the top. There will be a few individuals who feel or sense very little at first. As stated earlier, do not concern yourself with this situation. The technique is still affecting the subject as this vibration of sound works into the head, in particularly the pituitary gland. Some of the vibration will enter into the pineal gland, as well. It is subtle but effective in the long run.

Everyone is different and reacts to vibrations of sound and energy in varying ways. Be aware that not everyone you work with will experience the same physiological effects and sensations in the same manner. Some people experience these effects in different and unique ways. In any case, this is all part of each person's own spiritual growth.

Intoning or chanting the sound MAY has similar affects to toning AME, as in the first part of the Final Initiation discussed in chapter 1. Of course, the chart in chapter 2 that discusses the effects of the Final Initiation, can be referred to, if needed.

You can repeat the MAY chant again in the exact same manner, if you wish. This is entirely optional. In some cases, directing the sound toward your client a second time as she focuses on the white grape in the middle of the head again increases the sensations that were felt initially.

When you feel that you and your subject are ready, move on to the next technique, the Crown Chakra Opening and Clearing Technique. This should be a smooth transition for both you and your client.

As before, have her take in a deep breath and hold it for just a few seconds. Then the individual should release the breath evenly through the mouth or nose, followed by a return to normal breathing. Let your client imagine and feel warm water and sunlight moving from the white grape upward into the brain itself. The sunlight can also be pictured or felt as white light. The warm energy should continue to flow up through the brain, over the forehead. Let your subject feel this warm energy also moving up the back of the scalp. All of the warm energy should keep flowing up and into the top of the head in the crown chakra area. Guide the person gently but firmly.

Now, take in a deep breath yourself and hold it in the lungs for a very, brief moment. As you release the breath chant M-M-A-A-Y-Y. Concentrate on the client's head, especially the crown as you direct this sound toward the upper part of the head just above the forehead and ears.

Gaze about these areas as you release all your breath. Look at the energy or light about this area of the head as well as the crown. Take notice of the changes of the auric field about the head. You may be pleasantly surprised to observe that the aura has expanded outward from the head even more. More light and brightness has entered into the whole area. Darker colors or shading have disappeared around the edges of the human aura in this region.

Some of you may merely sense the changes here. Many of you may sense and see a lighter energy or manifestation of light about the crown, forehead and just above the ears. There will be a few of you who actually see pretty colors such as light blue, light green, white, and light yellow emanating within the aura in these areas. Any of these scenarios indicates that the technique is working for your client.

Now, ask your client to focus all her attention on the crown chakra directly at the top of the head. This is where the warmth or sensations should be situated. Again, step forward and place your two fingers, the index and middle ones, lightly onto the top of the head. Hold the fingers there for a few seconds and then pull them away. Put your hands either in your lap or down by your sides. Suggest to your client to focus on the pressure or sensation created by your fingers. Let her feel and sense that the fingers are still there.

Next, let the person see or sense the warmth or sensations spreading across the top of the head and scalp. This can be visualized as warm water and sunshine flowing outward. At this point, repeat the MAY chant in the same manner. This time focus all your attention on your patient or client's crown chakra as you release the sound vibrations. Feel the power in your voice as you expel all of your breath.

This breath and sound can be thought of as the Logos, or the word of the Creator. The ancient Egyptians recognized the power of the word and employed it in their rituals and ceremonies.

When you practice these techniques or do your own toning exercises, you are using this power. It is inherent in all of you.

Altogether the MAY chant should have been directed by you toward your subject three or four times. Of course, a total of four times indicated that you performed an additional chant during the White Grape Exercise. Think of the Law of Four in regards to this. Chanting three or four times in this manner creates the best results. The following analogy may help.

Imagine a car being stuck in the mud. The driver of the car steps on the gas pedal and causes the tires to spin. Unfortunately, the car remains stuck as the tires continue to turn with no results. Finally someone steps up to the back end of the vehicle. This person starts to push against the bumper or back end while the driver applies gas to the pedal again. As this person pushes a third time, the car breaks free of the mud. Chanting a sound or vibration three times works in the same way. Completing a fourth chant simply adds to the positive results.

Once you have completed the Crown Chakra Opening and Clearing Technique, you can either stop now or continue with the final exercise. This is your choice. If you decide to continue, you will find that the Warm Shower Technique is very effective and beneficial for your client or friend.

If you are proceeding make certain that your subject keeps the eyes shut through this technique, too. It should be an easy progression into this final technique.

Have your client take one more deep breath in and hold it for about three or four seconds. Then the breath should be released slowly. Ask your subject or client to return to normal breathing. Now, let your client continue to focus on the top of the head. As this is done, suggest that she is taking a very, warm shower. Let the person remember or feel the warm water of the shower cascading down upon the head. From this point, direct the flow of warm water over the head downwards. Use your voice to gently guide your client through this. Let the person sense or feel the warm soothing water trickling down the back and front of the head. The subject should also feel this energy flowing over the ears and down into the neck and shoulders.

Your friend or subject should now feel this warm water flowing from the top of the head and downwards over all of it. The energy should feel the same as a warm shower of water completely enveloping all of the head from the crown down to the upper chest and shoulders. Now, let this warm energy or water continue to move down into the chest as well as the upper back.

With a gentle but firm voice guide your client through this Warm Shower Technique. Focus on the flow of water coming down from above, onto the top of the head. Let your client feel and visualize this soothing energy completely surrounding him or her from the top of the head to the chest and upper back. Allow the person to feel and enjoy this technique for a few more moments.

Now, let your client feel the warm water moving down through the rest of the body. Let the individual feel or imagine the warm, sensations flowing or cascading down the spine, over the buttocks and down the back of the legs into the heels. Let her also feel this warm water showering down the front of the body, through the heart, solar, sacral, and base areas. Allow the flow to move down the thighs and finally into the feet.

Guide the warm water or energy through your client from the top of the head to the bottom of the feet. Keep suggesting that a warm shower of water is cascading from above the head, over the front and back of the body downward into the feet and heels. Do this for about a minute or two.

Finally, when you feel that you have guided your subject through the Warm Shower Technique long enough, stop. In order to do this, simply tell your client that the flow or water has stopped or turned off. At that point, ask your client to take in a deep breath and hold it for a few seconds. Then have her release the breath slowly. Instruct your client to open the eyes.

You have now completed the Warm Shower Technique along with the other techniques. You will probably notice or sense that the person sitting in front of you looks much more relaxed. The aura about the body and especially the head area appears or feels much larger and brighter to you. Once again, this is not your imagination. The client's aura is actually bigger and brighter because you have directed healing energy or Universal Energy through her aura, chakras and body.

When you and your client focus on warm water showering or flowing over the body, the healing energy enters into the crown chakra and flows in the same manner as water through the aura, chakras, and body. The person will feel more at peace and relaxed when you have finished guiding her through this special exercise as well as the other techniques.

Many of you will see or sense the light or colors flowing around the subject's head, face, chest, stomach, hips, and legs as you performed the Warm Shower Technique. After completing this guided meditation, you will probably still see this light or colors surrounding the individual. This indicates that healing energy from above is continuing to enter into the person's energy field and chakras. This may continue for a few moments afterwards.

Some of you may only sense or see some light around your subject. In this case the light will seem brighter and more expansive surrounding your subject. A few of you may not see anything at first. This is nothing to be concerned about. Although you may not see or sense any lights or colors please know that the technique is still working. Eventually, you will become more developed and start to see and sense all the beautiful light and colors about your clients or patients when you work with them. The more you practice the more you will awaken this gift.

After completing this and the other techniques just mentioned, you can begin your specific treatment or session with your client. You will find that the person will be more relaxed and receptive to the work you are about to do. If you are giving a Reiki treatment your subject will experience and enjoy the session even more. This is also true if you are giving a massage or doing reflexology on someone.

These special techniques enhance your treatments or sessions. Ultimately, you will become an even better healer or counselor. Your clients or patients and you will all benefit from these techniques.

As an "initiated" healer, counselor or teacher, you know that your purpose or mission in life is to be of service to others. This belief helps you to advance in your own spiritual growth.

The four elements consisting of earth, air, fire, and water were mentioned in an earlier chapter. These four elements are important and can be utilized in metaphysics and spiritual healing. In this chapter, chanting or intoning employed the air element in a special and spiritual way.

More advanced energy healing techniques including color healing will be covered in the next chapter.

"Doing good to others is not a duty. It is a joy, for it increases your own health and happiness."

—Zoroaster

Chapter 7

Advanced Energy Healing Techniques: Part Two

"Human energy is low and the Divine Energy is without limit. You are God. You are the Divine Energy. When you do the Divine work, your energy grows . . ."

—Sathya Sai Baba

In this chapter, advanced chakra energy techniques will be covered. Kundalini arousal techniques will also be taught in great detail.

The Human Chakra System

The human chakra system is important in regard to energy healing. There are approximately 130 chakras or energy centers existing within the human energy field. These centers are closely associated with the physical body. In the case of the major chakras, the glands, and organs of the endocrine system are closely linked to them.

These seven major energy centers can be activated to allow healing energy to flow through the aura, all of the chakras and into the body itself. This healing energy will work through the sympathetic nervous division and the central nervous system, too.

As stated, there is healing energy, Universal Energy or Divine Energy that exist in the heavenly realms. This energy consisting of very high vibrations will work its way down into the earthly realm. There are two ways that this occurs. Firstly, the old adage comes to mind, "as above, so below." In other words, what exists in the heavenly fields can exist in the earthly realm as well.In this situation, this energy consisting of a very high vibratory rate will flow downward from above and enter into the earthly realm. This healing energy sometimes referred to as chi or prana is present everywhere. It is in the air you breath, in the water you drink, and within the rocks and trees of the earth. However, this healing energy will have a slightly lower frequency or vibration when it is manifested here.

There are certain exercises you can do to draw in this high energy or chi. Deep breathing exercises such as the ones already covered in this book, is one method available to you. You can also pull the energy of the earth up into your body.

The second way that healing energy, Universal Energy or Divine Energy enters into the earthly realm is through you, in a very direct manner. Instead of drawing in this energy as just mentioned, you can have a direct channel to the Creator or Godsource and receive this high vibration of healing energy. The previous techniques covered in detail in the last chapter were designed with this in mind. When your crown chakra opens up it can access the divine or healing energy from above. The crown chakra, as it opens up, expands upward and connects to the eighth chakra.

The Eighth Chakra

The eighth chakra or energy center is part of the heavenly fields above. It is also a part of you. This chakra is located above the head at the upper edges of the crown energy center. It is approximately two feet above you and moves up and down according to the fluctuations of your auric field, especially the crown chakra. This special chakra is actually a doorway to the other side. It operates in a similar manner to a door being opened. When your crown chakra begins to open up you enter into a deep, altered state of consciousness. This allows your mind to become receptive to higher thoughts and energies.

As your crown chakra fully opens, it expands upward about two feet above the top of your head. This is where the eighth chakra is located. At this point, this eighth chakra or Divine Chakra opens up and joins with the upper edges of the crown energy center, which in turn opens up like a door. This event occurs when you are fully awakened and spiritually initiated. You are then linked or connected to the heavenly fields and energies above (see the following figure).

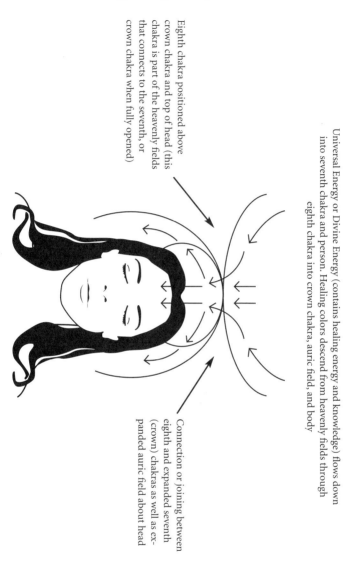

Eighth chakra positioned above crown chakra and top of head (this chakra is part of the heavenly fields that connects to the seventh, or crown chakra when fully opened)

Universal Energy or Divine Energy (contains healing energy and knowledge) flows down into seventh chakra and person. Healing colors descend from heavenly fields through eighth chakra into crown chakra, auric field, and body

Connection or joining between eighth and expanded seventh (crown) chakras as well as ex-panded auric field about head

Figure 7.1: Connection between the eighth chakra and the seventh, or crown chakra. Universal Energy, God, or Divine Energy, as well as healing colors, flow down into the crown center, aura, and body.

Being in an altered state allows your mind to be more receptive to higher energies and thoughts. Having the crown or seventh chakra open allows a direct connection to the Creator or Godsource by way of the eighth chakra. This was also referred to in chapter 6 in the Crown Chakra Opening and Clearing Technique.

Once the connection is made with the eighth chakra, many wonderful things can happen. It is through this special energy center that divine wisdom, knowledge, and information are received into your mind and ultimately the brain itself. This is why it is referred to as the Divine Chakra.

Once the crown is fully opened and connected to the eighth chakra, healing energy including healing colors, begin to flow downward. This energy along with these colors move from the eighth chakra into the crown chakra. From there these healing energies flow down into the aura and chakras. The healing colors and the healing or Universal Energy vibrates to a lower frequency and enters into both the central nervous system and the sympathetic nervous division. At this point, the healing energy, including the colors, move through the nerve meridians and into the body.

Chakra Energy Flow Techniques

You can open up the other main chakras or energy centers, as well as the crown chakra.

In *Ancient Teachings for Beginners,* chakra opening and flow techniques were explained in detail. This was done in order to help you safely and effectively open up your own energy centers, thereby releasing chakra energy. This energy is closely attuned to Universal Energy, chi, or Divine Energy.

In the following pages, you will be shown how to use these special techniques on someone else. Of course, these exercises can be tried on friends, family members and clients or patients. In particular, these Chakra Energy Flow Techniques should prove very effective on your client or patient base.

Once you have finished working on your client's crown chakra, you can focus on the other main chakras. In this case, the heart, solar, and sacral energy centers will be the three main chakras to work on. Occasionally, attention can be given to the throat and base chakras, as well.

Heart Chakra Opening and Flow Technique

You should begin by focusing on your client or subject's heart chakra. Move your eyes downward from the crown and face into the chest area. Have your client take in a deep breath and hold it for about five seconds. Then instruct her to release the breath slowly through the nose or mouth. Either way is fine. Leave this up to your subject. Let the individual return to normal breathing as you continue.

Next have your client put her hand onto the center of her chest. Try to have the person use the right hand for this exercise and for all the following exercises, if possible. This should be the rule even if your client is left-handed. There is a very simple reason for using the right hand in all of the chakra opening and flow techniques. The right side of the body, especially the right hand, contains the positive element of healing energy. This particular element or essence flows into the heart energy center and helps to activate this important chakra in a more effective manner.

However, if your subject feels more comfortable using her left hand, then let her do so. The negative element of healing energy or chi will still flow out the hand, palm, and fingertips into the chest area. This energy released through the left hand will help to activate the heart chakra. It will take a few seconds longer but will still be effective.

After your client has positioned the hand directly on top of the middle of the chest, you can guide her through the Heart Opening and Flow Technique. Make sure that the person's eyes remain shut during all of this.

Ask your client to concentrate on the hand and the warmth or pressure associated with it. As she does this, suggest that she is outside on a warm summer day. Let her feel, imagine or sense that the wonderful warmth of the sun is bathing her body and especially the chest. Ask her to feel the warmth beginning to penetrate through the skin and muscles of the chest. At the same time, let her feel the warmth or sensation of the hand spreading outwards over the chest and heart chakra.

Then, tell your client that the sun's rays and the warmth of the hand are penetrating together deep into the chest directly underneath the palm of the hand. Let this sensation or warmth penetrate about two to three inches below the surface of the skin. Allow your client to feel or sense these sensations pulsing from the hand and surface of the chest inwards. Let this pulsing and warm energy work deep within.

Now, have your client do one more deep breath exercise and then return to normal breathing. At this point, ask her to visualize or imagine a beautiful green flower, an orchid, all closed up inside the chest just below the palm of the hand. Let her feel or see this flower in the middle of the heart chakra. As the sun's warmth and the sensations of the palm penetrate inside the heart chakra, let her see or imagine the flower petals beginning to unfold. Allow your subject or client to enjoy these wonderful warm and pleasant sensations.

Then, let this person feel warm water within the center of the chest, in the middle of the green flower that represents the heart energy center. Guide the subject gently but firmly with your voice. Let the warm sensation of water spread across the heart chakra and chest. This should occur as the flower petals open up. Let your client feel or imagine both the petals and warm water spreading across the heart chakra. The expanding flower petals and water should spread through the heart, lungs, and ribs and also across the whole of the chest including the breasts and underarms. Direct this flow of warm water and unfolding flower petals completely across the heart energy center. The green flower petals should be fully opened. The warm water should also flow completely across this whole area, as well.

Ask your client how she feels. Find out if she feels or senses these sensations. You should always do a perception check with your client after this part of the Heart Chakra Opening and Flow Technique.

The results of this technique will vary with each individual. In most cases, the client will feel some warmth spreading through all or part of the chest. As well, some emotions such as anger, sadness, and pain may come to the surface. These negative emotions should disappear rather quickly and be replaced with warm, loving sensations as the subject's heart energy center opens up fully. However, the emotional release may not occur at this time. Your client may simply experience the pleasant warm sensation under the hand in the heart chakra and chest area.

In a few situations, the person may feel very little warmth or energy in the chest after doing the Heart Chakra Opening and Flow Technique. This is all right because the exercise is still working in a subtle manner. The heart chakra is starting to open more and will eventually open fully in the near future.

After checking with your subject, you can continue. Once again make sure that the client's eyes are shut. Guide her with the sound of your voice as you suggest that the warm sunshine and water is spreading all the way across her chest and into the shoulder and breasts. Let the person enjoy this experience for a few moments. If your client is not feeling as much, do not concern yourself with it. Simply, continue to guide her in this special exercise.

Once you have completed this heart chakra technique you can move on to the next technique.

Solar Plexus Chakra Opening and Flow Technique

As your client focuses on the heart chakra, suggest that both the warm water and sunshine are beginning to move downward over the breasts and into the stomach and solar plexus. Let her imagine it as warm, soothing water and sunshine flowing slowly downward until the energy is centered just above the navel.

Next, have the individual move her hand down to the solar plexus, placing it firmly onto the surface of this center. Make sure that it is positioned about two to three inches above the belly button directly in the middle of the stomach area.

This time as you instruct your client to take in a deep breath, have her draw it into the diaphragm. This type of breathing ensures that the air filled with the chi or Universal Energy enters into the lower part of the lungs, diaphragm and solar plexus. This helps to activate the solar plexus chakra. Let her hold the breath for about three or four seconds. Then tell her to release the breath slowly either through the nose or mouth and return to normal breathing.

A similar procedure as the heart chakra technique should be followed when working with the solar energy center. Your client should now focus all her attention on her solar plexus and the palm of her hand.

Tell her to feel the warmth or pressure of the hand upon the surface of the solar plexus. Let her feel this warmth or sensation penetrating through the skin until it is about two or three inches beneath the palm of her hand.

Then, have your subject picture or imagine a beautiful yellow flower positioned here, just below the surface of the skin. You can even suggest that it is a specific flower such as a daffodil or tulip, if you think this will help your client to visualize the yellow flower easier.

As she concentrates on this flower, guide her with the warm sun meditation that you just used during the Heart Opening and Flow Technique. Let her sense or see the yellow flower petals beginning to open as the warm rays of the sun penetrate through the skin into this area of the stomach.

Allow your client to feel, see or imagine the beautiful petals spreading quickly across the solar plexus. Along with the flowers unfolding, let the flow of warm water spread across this area. Allow the warm water and opening petals to completely spread through the stomach, internal organs, solar plexus muscles, and the surface directly under the palm of the hand. Let this warm energy flow completely through the solar plexus center. Even the warmth or pressure of the palm, thumbs and fingers should be felt. Let this healing energy flow out the ends of the finger and thumbs into the solar plexus. Your subject should experience this energy flowing all the way across the surface of the skin.

Tell her to feel and sense the flower petals fully opened and expanded all the way across the stomach from side to side. Let the client enjoy the warmth and pleasant feeling flowing inside the stomach and across the solar plexus. Have her concentrate on this for a few minutes. Keep mentioning that warm water and sunshine is flowing across the stomach. Use words such as "relaxing" and "soothing" to reinforce the experience. You have now completed the Solar Plexus Opening and Flow Technique.

At this time you can make a decision whether or not to do a perception check on your client. If she appears very relaxed and you sense or see a white light surrounding her head area, then it is best not to check with her. Let her be.

You might also notice some white light around the palm of her hand, the chest and both breasts. This is another indication that your client is responding well to the techniques. She is very relaxed and the Divine Energy or Universal Energy, along with the chakra energy, is working into her body.

This healing energy has now moved through the crown chakra, over the throat chakra and into the heart chakra. Soon this energy will begin to move through the rest of the main chakras and body.

It is now time to move on to the next technique.

Sacral Chakra Opening and Flow Technique

Instruct your client to move her hand down from the solar plexus chakra onto the sacral plexus chakra. Her hand should be placed on top of the sacral directly in the middle about two inches below the navel. Once she has positioned the palm of her hand here, you can guide her in moving the energy down from the solar energy center into the sacral energy center.

Use the same method that was used to move the energy from the heart center to the solar plexus center. Guide her firmly but gently. This should be a smooth progression from one chakra to another.

Let her feel the warmth of the sun and water flowing down across the navel area and into the sacral where the hand is positioned. Allow this warm, soothing sensation to move into the sacral plexus chakra just beneath the palm of the hand. Instruct your client to focus all her attention on this area. Then, have her take in another deep breath. This time she should imagine that the breath or chi is going into the sacral energy center instead of the chest or solar plexus.

Let her hold it for a few seconds and then release it as before. Have the client return to normal breathing.

As she concentrates on her hand suggest that a beautiful, orange flower is closed up underneath this area. Tell your client to visualize or sense this flower here directly beneath the palm of her hand. Once again, use the suggestion of warm sunshine penetrating through the hand, the skin and sacral chakra. She should also feel the warmth or pressure of the palm of her hand at the same time. Even the warmth or sensations of the thumb and fingertips should be focused on. Let her feel the energy of the hand and the warmth of the sun penetrating beneath the surface of the skin to a depth of about two inches. This is where the orange flower should be situated. The sensations of the palm of the hand and the sun should flow inwards until they touch the closed-up flower within.

Guide her in the same manner as you did through the Solar Plexus Chakra Opening and Flow Technique. Let her see and feel the orange flower petals unfolding as the warmth of the sun and hand enters here. Use a firm, steady voice as you suggest to her that the flower petals are rapidly spreading underneath the palm of the hand and across the sacral. As you do this also tell her that warm water and sunshine are beginning to flow across this area. Allow the warm water and sunshine to completely spread across the sacral plexus at the same time as the unfolding flower petals. The orange flower petals should unfurl until they are completely opened from hip to hip. Tell her to feel the wonderful, sensations flowing across here, as well.

Let your client enjoy the warmth of the sun and water spreading across the sacral. In fact, these sensations should also be felt deep inside. Suggest to your subject that the healing energy of the sun and water have penetrated deep within all the internal organs.

If your client has problems with the ovaries, this particular exercise will help to send healing energy directly into this organ. Conversely, a male client will also benefit from this procedure in regard to prostate problems.

Your client should be allowed to enjoy this part of the Sacral Chakra Opening and Flow Technique for a few minutes. The chances are that she will be in a very deep altered state of consciousness by the time that you complete this technique. This ensures that the energy flows through her aura, chakras, body and organs. After this you can move on to the next technique that connects with this one.

Base Chakra Opening and Flow Technique

There are two options that you can use when you start this technique. The first option involves your client keeping her hand placed on the sacral plexus. In this case, the warmth and energy in the sacral chakra and the fingertips can be harnessed.

Tell your client to feel this warm sensation beginning to move down from the fingertips and sacral into the base energy center. Suggest that warm water and sunshine is flowing down from the sacral into the base. By using this option, the warmth from the palm, thumb, and fingertips will flow on its own accord into the base chakra. The activated sacral chakra will also release energy that will move down into this lower chakra.

The second option that can be employed involves having your client move the hand down to the base energy center. In this case, the palm of the hand should be positioned directly on top of this area. This alternative method can be used if your subject feels comfortable with it and you believe it will be beneficial. In any event, either option will work effectively. The first method mentioned is the one that will be used most often.

Once you have directed the warm sensations of the sun and water into her base center, ask her to focus all her attention here. Let her feel the warmth flowing from the fingertips into this area along with the sun and water. Or if using the second method, she should feel the warmth and slight pressure of the palm of the hand working under the skin into this energy center.

Next, your subject should visualize a beautiful red rose closed up within the base. She should concentrate on this red flower for a few seconds, continuing to feel the warm sensations flowing through here. As before, guide her through the opening of the beautiful flower petals. As the sun and water flows into this red rose, the petals will unfold steadily across the base chakra. At the same time, she should feel the warmth of the sun and water spreading across here. Allow her to do this until the red flower petals are coming unfurled from upper thigh to upper thigh. The warm sensations of the water and sun should also be felt fully through this area, including the hips.

Let your client enjoy this wonderful feeling for several seconds. You have now completed the Base Chakra Opening and Flow Technique.

By this time, your subject or client should be extremely relaxed and feeling warm sensations within. All seven of the major chakras or energy centers have been activated and opened up to their full potentials. The chakra energy from each center along with the Divine Energy or Universal Energy from above has been released and allowed to flow through your clients' aura, chakras, body, and nervous center. In this situation, these energies have flowed from the crown to the base chakra.

You can make a choice at this point to either end this guided chakra meditation or continue with the next phase of this special energy work. If you decide to continue guiding her through the techniques then the next step will be a natural progression.

Prior to discussing the next step, a few things must be discussed in regard to the base chakra and kundalini. One of the physiological affects associated with the activation and opening of the base or root chakra is the release of kundalini. This is sometimes referred to as "serpent power" or "the fire within." Kundalini is a Sanskrit word meaning "coiled serpent." It is aptly named.

This serpent power is stored near the lower end of the spine between the anus and the reproductive organs. When the base energy center opens up it can sometimes send energy, including chakra energy, into this area. The result is the activation or arousal of this incredible energy. The serpent power or kundalini once aroused will begin to flow up through the body, the spine, and the chakras. It will work its way out the top of the head where the crown chakra is located. This stored energy can either flow up to the crown in a slow, methodical manner or in a powerful rush. If you can think of a volcanic eruption, you will understand how quickly the energy can flow.

As the serpent power awakens and begins to move, it can sometimes flow down the thighs and out the bottoms of the feet as well. In this case, the client or subject will feel incredible warmth in her thighs. It will feel as if the thighs and possibly the legs are on fire. Your client may even feel the same sensations moving up the chakras and body into the top of the head. Hence, the term "the fire within."

By performing all the special chakra opening and flow techniques just described, you can prepare your client to work with this wonderful energy in a safe and effective manner. You can train the person to direct this energy up through her own body and spine safely and in a proficient way. If taught properly, your client will become adept at working with kundalini on a regular basis.

There are many benefits associated with the use of this serpent energy. It is great for the reduction of stress, the slowing down of the aging process, the balancing of the endocrine glandular system and the release of healing energy into areas of the body where it is required. Spiritual advancement and psychic development is also a direct result of working with the kundalini and the chakras. You are now ready to move on to the next step.

The Crown-to-Base Energy Flow Technique

Upon completion of the Base Chakra Opening and Flow technique, you can begin to move the chakra energy, including the kundalini up through your client's body, spine, and chakras in a slow, deliberate way.

Begin the process by letting your client focus for a few more moments on the warm sensations in the base energy center. Then guide the warm water and sunshine up from the base into the sacral chakra. The warm flow of energy should spread completely across the sacral from hip to hip.

Your subject should experience this for a few seconds as you keep suggesting that warm water and sunshine is flowing across this area and also deep within the organs of the sacral area. As this happens, the orange flower petals should open up once more in a much quicker manner. Once opened, these petals, as well as other petals associated with each specific chakra, should remain opened during this special energy flow technique. Eventually, each opened flower, representing their respective chakra, will begin to close up on its own. This happens after completion of the Crown to Base Energy Flow Technique.

Now, continue guiding her gently with your voice. Let her feel the warm energy starting to move upward again. This time continue over the belly button and along both sides until the wonderful warmth of the water and sunshine has flowed into the solar plexus chakra. As before, make the suggestion to your client that flower petals are opening up. In this case, yellow flower petals will be used. The warm energy should be felt deep inside the stomach and internal or-

gans located within the solar energy center. These warm
sensations should flow all the way across the skin until these
sensations exist from side to side.

As before, your subject should enjoy these wonderful,
soothing feelings for a brief moment. Then continue the
guiding process. Move the warm water and sunshine upward again.

Think of this process as connecting the dots. In this
case, the major energy centers represent these dots. As the
flow of warm energy moves from the base upward into
each chakra, a connection or joining of the major chakras
begin to take place.

Allow this pleasant energy to flow over the breasts and
into the chest and heart chakra. Have her focus her attention
on this area and feel the warmth spreading across the chest.
This warmth should also be felt spreading deep inside. She
should experience the warm sensations flowing across the
ribs, tendons, heart, lungs, and thymus gland. Of course, this
important gland is located in the upper part of the chest and
associated with the immune system of the body.

Say that the warm water and sunshine is flowing into
her shoulders and even underneath the arms. Have the person picture or sense the green flower petals unfolding as before. This time the flower petals are opening quicker until
they are fully unfurled across your client's chest, breast, and
shoulders.

The client should enjoy this experience for a few seconds as well. You may notice or sense a white light or energy in the heart chakra as you direct her through this part
of the Crown to Base Chakra Energy Flow Technique.

Continue the meditation by directing the warm sensations of the sun and water upward again. The warm energy should move up into the neck and throat chakra. It should also move up the back of the neck into the base of the skull at the same time. Keep suggesting that a flow of warm water and sunshine is flowing steadily upward.

A beautiful blue flower located in the throat area should also be seen or imagined by the subject as the warmth passes through here. Let the flower petals open fully from one side of the throat to the other side.

From here, allow the sensations or energy to spread up into the face, over the eyes and into the third eye chakra. She should feel warm water and sunshine spreading completely across the brow until it encompasses the forehead, from temple to temple.

Once again, you can employ another flower opening exercise. This purple flower should completely open up across the brow until it spreads from temple to temple, as well. She should focus on the third eye area for a few seconds. There is a chance that the person may feel a pulsing or throbbing sensation within the middle of the forehead as she concentrates on the energy here. These types of physiological sensations are normal and indicate that the pineal gland is opening up more. This ensures that your subject's third eye activates and opens up fully, too. As she experiences the sensations within the brow and third eye chakra, she should also feel warmth in the back of the head.

Now, continue the meditation. With a firm, steady voice tell her to feel and see the warm water and sunshine flowing upward again. Let these feelings move up the front and back of the head simultaneously. These soothing sensations should flow completely up to the top of the head where the crown energy center is located.

Once you have directed the energy to the top of the head, step forward and touch this area with two fingers. Hold the fingers lightly on the scalp for about two seconds and then remove your fingers from the crown chakra. This is a repeat of the original exercise that involves the opening of the crown chakra as mentioned in the last chapter.

It is now time for you to direct the warm rays of the sun into the top of the head. As the individual focuses on this area, tell her that the sun is beating down upon her head. Suggest to her that the warmth of the sun is penetrating through the top of the scalp, through the hair, and into the upper part of the head itself.

In the last chapter, a white rose was used as part of the Crown Opening and Clearing Technique. This exercise will be used again. This time the beautiful rose petals are partially opened. Let her imagine the sun striking the rose that is situated near the top of the head. It should be visualized about one inch under the surface of the scalp. As this occurs the partially opened white petals start to unfold even more. Your client should feel the warmth and sensations spreading through the top of the head as the flower petals open up completely. In this case, the white rose petals should be able to open up much more quickly than the first time.

The flower petals, along with the warm energy of the sun, should fully encompass the entire top, back and sides of the head. The client should focus all attention here for a few seconds and enjoy the meditation.

Now, ask your client to feel or imagine that she is taking a very, warm shower. Let the warm water shower down upon the crown and top of her head. Suggest to her that the warm water is flowing all over the head, down the back of the neck and over her forehead.

Then begin the important process of directing this flow of water downward. Let her feel the water moving down over the eyebrows, face, throat, and into the chest. From here, direct the warm water throughout the heart chakra and completely across the chest. Once more, tell your subject that the green flower petals are opening up and expanding. This time, the flower petals should open up more quickly as the sensation of water spreads throughout the heart energy center, up into the shoulders and breasts. Mention to her that the warm water is flowing into the heart, lungs, and ribs in a healing and soothing manner.

Using your voice in these guided meditation techniques is very important for the following reasons. You develop the ability to calm and relax others such as clients, patients and friends. This helps with the reduction of stress in the lives of people around you. Also, this allows your relaxed client or subject to enter into a deeper state of consciousness. As this occurs her brain wave patterns slow down even more. She is then more receptive to your suggestions and energy directing. Your voice coupled with your concentration becomes powerful.

In essence, you are actually starting to direct and move the chi or healing energy through your subject's aura, chakras, and physical body. This is a wonderful gift to give. Awareness of this will help you to realize the power associated with the voice, the human chakra system, and the Universal Energy or healing energy. All have the potential to heal.

Now, move the warm water and energy from your client's heart chakra and chest down into the solar plexus chakra. Let her feel this pleasant sensation as a warm shower of water over this part of the body. The water should spread all the way across the surface of the skin and deep into the internal organs. As before, she should see and sense the yellow flower petals opening up completely across the solar plexus chakra. These petals will probably unfold faster this time as she focuses on this area.

She should feel the wonderful warmth and energy here for a brief moment. Then, direct the warm water downward again, past the belly button and into the sacral. Let her feel it moving slightly faster as it flows over and alongside the navel and finally into the sacral plexus located about two or three inches below.

As the warm sensation of water flows into this energy center, tell your client to see and feel the beautiful orange flower petals opening up quickly until they encompass this area from hip to hip. The warm water should also be felt deep within the internal organs of the sacral plexus.

When the energy is directed here in this manner, the sacral chakra activates and opens up. This allows the energy contained within this center to be released. As this happens this energy joins with the healing or Universal Energy and works together in harmony.

This is particularly beneficial for female clients who have certain problems with the ovaries. For instance, symptoms of menopause can be lessened or alleviated when energy work is focused here on a regular basis. Also, women facing hormonal and physiological changes associated with pre-menopause can slow down the inevitable.

For both men and women, the activation of the sacral chakra, sometimes referred to as the sexual chakra, can increase the desire for sex. This is important for individuals suffering from a low sex drive. Obviously, a healthy sexual appetite adds to the enjoyment of life. These are three prime examples of the benefits associated with stimulating this chakra.

Once your client has felt the warm, pleasant feelings here for a few seconds, move it downward again. The warm water should flow into the base or root chakra. Tell her that it is penetrating into the beautiful red rose located here. In this instance, the rose petals will be opened slightly as she concentrates on this center. These petals should unfold faster this time as the warm energy moves into the base chakra. This pleasant energy should be felt deep within the base and spread across the upper thighs.

When the client has experienced this for a brief moment, you will then be ready to direct the energy upward once more. In this case, the chi or energy represented as warm water should be directed in a faster manner. Think of it flowing in one fluid motion.

Now, speed up the momentum of your voice slightly as you direct your client. Do keep your voice gentle, though. Suggest to her that the soothing water is flowing up at a quicker and stronger rate. Let it move into the sacral chakra again. As it does, the energy will spread rapidly across this center and through the fully opened flower petals, as well.

Instead of focusing on the sacral energy center for a few moments, direct the warm water up over the navel and into the solar plexus chakra. Have your client sense the energy spreading across the stomach area and throughout this energy center. The yellow flower petals will be fully opened during this time. Allow the warm energy to flow through these petals, too. Always use the words "warm water" and "energy" as you direct your subject.

Once more, in a steady but gentle voice, guide the energy upward over the breasts and into the heart chakra in the middle of the chest. Tell her to feel or sense the water flowing completely across the chest as before. The warm water should flow quickly through the green flower petals that are fully opened from armpit to armpit. This healing energy can be felt up into both shoulders, also.

Continue the guided meditation by letting the warm energy or water move into the upper part of the chest, through the throat chakra, the neck and onto the face. Say that it is flowing upward in one smooth motion. The client should experience this pleasant sensation moving across the face, over the closed eyes and into the third eye chakra once again. In this case, the beautiful purple flower petals can be visualized or sensed as being fully open. These petals will spread from temple to temple.

Remind the client to feel the slight pressure of your two fingers touching here again. Even though your fingertips are not placed on the forehead this time, she will probably perceive this sensation. Allow her to feel the warm water spreading across the brow as well as through the opened flower. This energy should be felt within the third eye chakra about an inch below the surface of the skin.

Now, direct this healing energy, recognized as water deep into the center of the head. At this moment, tell her to experience the warm water moving up the brow, over the scalp and onto the top of the head. Simultaneously, let her sense the warm energy moving up the brain and into the top of the head as well. Let your client focus on this for just a brief moment.

You are now ready to move this energy back down through the person's body and chakras. Suggest to your client she is taking a very warm shower again. She should visualize and feel the warm water showering down on her body. This water will flow from above the crown chakra, onto the top of the head and down over the face. It should also shower down the back of the head, neck and over the upper back.

Keep the momentum by directing the energy in a continuous fashion. Let her feel the flow of warm water moving past the chin, onto the throat and then into the heart chakra. Ask her to feel love and warmth within her heart as the energy flows here. If you feel it is necessary, she can focus on a loved one for a brief second. From the chest and heart chakra, the water should move downward over the breast, into the solar plexus again. Allow it to spread rapidly across this area from side to side.

Next, in a smooth and steady voice, direct the warm water past both sides of the belly button into the sacral chakra. Mention that the warm sensations are spreading throughout this energy center. As before, the energy should spread completely through the flower petals that are opened from hip to hip.

Then let the energy or warm water flow down into the base energy center. As it does remind your client that the red rose petals are fully opened from thigh to thigh. The pleasant feelings of warm water should be experienced here for a second or two. The client may even feel this as a warm, pulsing sensation deep within the base chakra.

At this point, you can now direct this wonderful energy up the person's body and chakras at a faster, smoother pace. You will not need to mention the different colored flowers this time.

Keep in mind that you are moving or directing both kundalini and chi up at the same time. This is powerful energy that can heal and soothe your client on a physical and spiritual level.

Say that the warm water is flowing up as one fluid motion. Ask her to picture it as a fountain of water flowing upward from the base. This water will move over the sacral, over the navel, into the solar plexus, and over both breasts. It will spread like warm water over the entire chest and flow quickly up the throat and face. Keep it moving over the forehead, into the scalp and finally the top of the head. Ask your subject to feel warm water showering or pulsing here in the crown chakra.

Then, direct this warm water down the front of the face and down the back of the head at the same time. Suggest that the warm shower is cascading down over the head and down the body. Let the flowing water begin to rush downward over the chest, solar, sacral, and into the base chakra. Have it shower down over the neck, the back and into the buttocks and tail bone or sacrum at the same time.

As soon as you have directed the energy into the base as well as the sacrum direct the warm water upward once again. Mention the warm water fountain once more. Tell the client or patient to feel the water rushing up the body, over the sacral, solar, and into the heart center. Let her sense the fountain of water moving up the spine, through the middle of the back and into the upper back and shoulders, too. From here, direct the warm water up over the face and the back of the neck simultaneously. Allow the energy to continue upward, over the forehead and back of the head until it flows to the top of the head itself.

Congratulations! You have now succeeded in directing Universal Energy and kundalini through your subject in a safe and effective manner. This ability will become greater as you practice these special techniques more.

Now, that the energy is flowing in a fast, fluid manner, you must continue the process.

This time your client should visualize the shower of water starting to surround her body as it works downward. If she can imagine herself taking a warm shower this will help. Let this powerful flow of energy move over the front and back of the body downward. Keep telling her that the water is rushing down over the chest, solar, sacral, and into the base. At the same time the warm flowing water should rush down the spine and into the buttocks, as before.

Then have her see and feel the energy rushing upward through the front and back of the body. When the energy arrives at the crown again, simply direct it back down. Let the warm water that represents the energy move quickly to the base chakra and sacrum.

Have the water flow up again to the top of the head. Tell your client that the warm water and energy is moving rapidly up and down through the chakras and body including the spine. Let it keep flowing up and down the body, the major chakras and back. As this energy moves through your client, tell her that it is moving and pulsing very quickly.

Observe her face while doing this. You may notice rapid eye movement below her closed eyelids. In some cases, the eyes will move up and down in the same direction as the flow of water. This indicates two things. First of all, your client is in a deeply altered state of consciousness. Secondly, she is concentrating fully on the warm energy moving rapidly through the chakras and body.

You can direct the flow of warm water up and down the body three or four more times. This will allow the client to enjoy this wonderful experience for a few more moments. In essence, you have successfully guided your client or subject through most of the Crown-to-Base Energy Flow Technique.

A determination can be made at this time whether to continue onto the next step or to finish off the exercise. Observe your client and use your own inner guidance. If you feel that this is enough work for now, then you can use your voice in an effective manner to slow down and finally stop the energy, including the kundalini, from flowing. This will be explained shortly.

It is a smooth transition to the next step, if you decide to continue.

The Water Fountain and Feet Chakra Technique

In the last technique a warm water fountain was referred to very briefly. This was done in order to help your client feel the kundalini and energy more effectively. This imagery method will be used once more for this special technique.

As stated previously, you can guide the warm water through your subject about three or four more times. Then, as the energy is directed into the base chakra, move it downward instead. Guide the water down the legs. Tell her that the warm water is flowing down the thighs, the knees and into the feet.

When the water flows into both feet, mention the water fountain. This time, it is situated directly beneath. Have her visualize the fountain splashing and bubbling. Then, tell her to see and sense the warm water rushing upward through the legs. Let it flow quickly up the front and back of the body. This energy should rush through all the major chakras as well as the spine. It will continue upward in a rapid motion. Allow the warm water to flow over the face, the back of the head, and into the top of the head.

Have the water rush back down again into the feet. As it reaches the feet, let it rush back up. When it gets to the crown chakra once more, direct it down through the front and back of the body.

With a steady voice, keep guiding the water up and down the client's chakras and whole body. Pay particular attention to the light or illuminations surrounding the person. Watch the face, too. You will probably notice that the face looks brighter, calmer, and more at peace.

Let your client or patient experience this healing energy for a few minutes. After this period of time, you can start to wind down the guided meditation.

This is a very simple process to follow.

Using your voice, have your client feel and see the warm flow of water slowing down as it moves up and down her body. Instruct her to consciously focus on this warm energy. As she does this, allow the water to slow down even more. Let the client or patient experience this energy as it slows. Let her focus on the warm water moving slowly through each major chakra as well as through the legs. The flow from the water fountain is becoming less and less every time it moves up the legs and through the entire body.

Finally, suggest that the water has decreased to a trickle. Then, let the energy stop in either the crown or heart chakra. You decide where to stop this energy flow. Either chakra is fine. It is simply your choice.

Once you have completed this slowing down process, you and your subject can relax for a few moments. Tell her to take in one more deep breath and then release it evenly through the mouth or nose. She should return to normal breathing afterwards. Allow her to sit or lie there for a minute until she returns to normal consciousness. You have now completed all the chakra energy flow techniques with your client or subject.

If you check with your subject after finishing these techniques, you will probably find that the person feels much lighter and more at peace. Physical pain in the body may be lessened too. The client's auric field should look much brighter and expanded. If you cannot see her aura, you may sense it instead. In any case, the energy and color of the aura should be much improved after performing these special procedures with her. You may notice that the individual's eyes seem brighter and the face appears more relaxed.

These are all signs that the chakra energy techniques have worked on your client. These same techniques can be taught to the client as well.

Practice these special exercises until you become comfortable with them. Eventually you will be able to direct energy through clients or patients in an easy and smooth manner. You will also develop a power in the voice to direct and influence them in a positive way when you do guided meditations.

When you feel you are ready, you can add the following step of teaching these techniques to your clients. Simply have your client concentrate on the crown or heart energy center after you have completed the energy work.

Ask the client to see and feel the warm water showering down from above the head. Let her move this warm energy slowly down the body like taking a very warm shower. Tell her to feel the water moving through the face, the heart chakra, the solar, sacral and into the base chakra. Mention to her that it is like connecting the dots.

As she moves this warm flow of water into the base, have her focus here for a brief moment. Then, she should feel and see the warm water flowing back up her body until it reaches the top of her head.

Once again, tell her to feel the shower of warm water pouring over the top of the head and crown chakra. Let her move the warm water or energy back down her body, through all her chakras into her base again. Suggest that the water is flowing down her back into the buttocks, too.

Now, have her move this energy up as one fluid motion. It should flow rapidly and evenly up the front and back of the body into the crown chakra area. As it reaches the top of the head, tell her to concentrate on sending this warm water back down again into the base.

Your client should repeat this process two or three more times. All the time, the energy should be moved faster and faster through her body. She can concentrate on doing this as she sends the warm energy through the chakras and body. Then, as the warm water flows into the base chakra your client should direct it down both thighs, past the knees and into the bottom of the feet.

At this time, she should employ the Water Fountain and Feet Chakra Technique. Mention the warm water fountain to her and tell her to let it flow up through the legs into the base energy center.

From the base, your patient or client should direct the warm water fountain up the body, through the major chakras, up the back and into the top of the head. Let her feel the warm sensations on the scalp for a few seconds.

She can then focus on the warm water showering down over the head, the face through the energy centers and spine. As the water or energy arrives into the base, your client should move it rapidly down the legs and into the feet.

The person can keep the momentum by having the fountain of warm water rush up the legs, into the base, through the major chakras and spine, and onto the top of the head. You can have your subject continue doing this several more times.

Simply guide her with your voice. Tell her to move this warm energy or water up and down the body, from the top of the head to the bottom of the feet and back up again.

When you feel that your client has done enough energy work, tell her to consciously focus on the water. As she does this, she should concentrate on slowing the flow down.

Instruct her to see and feel this water becoming slower and slower as it moves through her body. Finally, have her stop the energy in either her heart energy center or her crown energy center. Leave this up to your subject.

When she is finished, let her take in a deep breath as before. Have her hold it for a few seconds. Then she can release it slowly and evenly out the mouth or nose. Let her relax here for a brief moment before she returns to normal awareness. You may need to tell her to feel herself back in the room. Then instruct her to open her eyes.

Once your client has successfully employed these energy techniques on herself, she can practice them anytime she wants. The more that she practices, the better she will become at moving Universal Energy, chakra energy and kundalini through her own body. This is a wonderful ability to develop.

The capability of directing energy through your own body and chakras allows you to slow down your aging process and reduce stress in your life. The auric field becomes bright and expanded. The human chakra system becomes balanced and maintains a healthy flow of energy through the chakras, the nervous system, the cells, the glands, and the organs of the physical body. Psychic and spiritual abilities become greatly enhanced.

As well as doing energy flow techniques on yourself, you can employ it on your clients and others for positive benefits. If you are capable of directing energy through other people you should become quite adapt at moving it through yourself, too. In essence, you feel more alive and contented by doing your own energy work.

There is one other benefit to all of this special energy work. Eventually, as you become confident and proficient at moving energy through your clients or patients, you will automatically move the energy through yourself at the very same time. In other words, when your client feels the warm water or energy flowing through her body, you will experience the same sensations. The sensations for you may be less dramatic but will be felt nonetheless. This ensures that you maintain your own harmony, health, and balance.

It was mentioned previously that there are four elements. These are earth, air, fire, and water. Throughout this chapter some of these elements of nature were employed. The understanding of the mystical value of these four elements should become more apparent as you use them in your own healing work.

Deep breathing exercises were used during these energy flow techniques. Of course, this is a representation of the air element. Water visualization exercises were also employed. This is a use of the water element. So two of the four elements were used extensively throughout this chapter. This shows the importance and mystical value of the four elements of nature.

The ability to move energy through others or through your self is a great gift. It allows you to become a better healer, teacher, or counselor. Your psychic and spiritual gifts become stronger. It helps you to become spiritually enlightened or initiated. This ensures that your life will flow in a more productive and harmonious way. A spiritual path leads you back to the Creator. This is the goal that you should strive to attain.

Finally, it should be mentioned that there are other wonderful benefits associated with doing these types of energy techniques. You can use the Chakra Flow Techniques to train yourself to do soul traveling. These can also help you to receive past-life recall. As well, important information and wisdom can be received.

Become confident in doing energy work and enjoy your spiritual journey.

> "Nothing in life is to be feared, it is only to be understood."
>
> —Marie Curie

Chapter 8

Working with Healing Colors

> "Limited in his nature, infinite in his desires, man
> is a fallen god who remembers the heavens."
>
> —Alphonse De Lamartine

Healing colors were mentioned in the previous chapter. It was explained that these colors flow downward from the heavenly fields through the eighth chakra and into the seventh or crown chakra. Along with these special colors, Universal Energy or healing energy flows into the crown center, as well.

These colors are closely connected to the Universal or Divine Energy. They have an extremely high vibratory rate. People with the ability to see auras and higher energies can see and sense these beautiful illuminations.

Each of these colors has its own rate of vibration or frequency. These colors, ranging from the lowest frequency to the highest, are red, orange, yellow, green, light blue, indigo or mid-blue, violet or light purple, gold, and white. To a person who sees auras and higher energies, these illuminations appear similar to the colors found in a rainbow.

When you employ the special energy techniques described in the last chapter, the healing colors just listed will flow into the client along with the Universal Energy. This allows the potential for true healing to occur.

People suffering from certain illnesses can benefit from this. This happens because the high vibration of healing energy associated with these special colors work into the body in the following manner.

It was explained previously that the healing colors and Universal Energy flow into the crown chakra as it opens up. These energies come from the eighth chakra and heavenly fields above. As the healing colors and chi enter into the crown energy center, they will move downward through the aura and chakras. During all of this, these high vibrations of energy will step down to lower frequencies.

As the colors and Universal Energy flow into the major chakras, they will work into the Sympathetic Nervous Division and Central Nervous System. It is here that the stepping-down process or the lowering of these frequencies takes place. When these colors and healing energy vibrate at a slightly lower frequency, these energies will flow through both the Central Nervous System and Sympathetic Division. These colors and chi will move out the nerve meridians and energy meridians into the body. Both the nerve and energy meridians are in close proximity to one another.

Healing colors, along with Universal Energy or chi, will flow through both the nerve and energy meridians into the glands, organs, cells, and tissues of the human body. This ensures that high vibrations of healing colors and energy affect these areas of the body in a beneficial way. In essence, the healing color along with the healing energy will raise the vibrations of these areas. The following example should be given in order to give you a better understanding of the procedure.

If a woman is suffering from the first stages of breast cancer, her auric field will contain a dirty light-yellow color within. This unpleasant or unwanted color will exist above the breast where the disease is located. When the healing colors and Universal Energy enters into her aura, chakras, and body in the manner just described, they will flow into the affected area. In this particular case, it will be the breast.

The colors along with the chi will start to affect the negative color situated over the breast. These colors, especially green and light blue, will join with the dirty-yellow lumination and begin to change to a cleaner and lighter color. A medical intuitive or aura reader witnessing this will actually see the change occurring before their eyes. It will appear as light-blue and green mist moving over the face into the chest, and finally into the discoloration above the diseased area. The aura reader should see the colors, especially the green and blue beginning to swirl around and within the dirty-yellow color.

This woman who has the first stages of breast cancer, will probably feel tingling energy or a coolness occurring in the breast as this happens. This is an indication that the energy treatment is working. The person is feeling healing energy and healing colors entering into the diseased cells and tissues.

Now, if this person continues to do her own energy work, the healing energies will keep flowing into the affected area. Both the healing colors and the Universal Energy will change the vibrations or frequencies of the diseased cells and tissues. Eventually, these cells and tissues will become balanced and healthy.

This process just mentioned can also work on other diseases and disorders. Arthritis, other cancers, and illnesses can be affected in a very positive way when energy techniques are employed. Either a person can do her own energy work or else a healer can practice these techniques on the client or patient. In each situation, the potential for true healing is available.

Eventually, medical science will recognize the true value of working with higher vibrations of energy. This includes Reiki, Therapeutic Touch, hands-on healing, chakra energy work and distance healing.

It must be remembered that everything vibrates at different rates or frequencies. For instance, it is believed that the earth itself vibrates at 7 cps or Hertz, as it is called in physics. If something vibrates at its proper frequency, then harmony and balance occurs. However, if something such as an organ or cell has the wrong rate of vibration or frequency, disease can occur within this cell or organ.

When someone does energy work on herself or somebody else, high vibrations of healing energy will affect the physical, emotional, and spiritual levels of the person involved. These energies, including healing colors, can slow down aging, reduce or eliminate pain, and in some cases, heal the early stages of disease. The results vary for each individual. There are many variables connected with energy healing.

The Divine Intelligence of the Creator or Godsource influences the outcome in many situations. If a person afflicted with a life-threatening disease decides that he or she does not wish to live anymore, than this decision can affect the healing process. In this case, the individual on a higher level connects with this Divine Intelligence. This starts the process of death or transition for the sufferer. As a result, the person will pass over despite any attempts at energy work or medical treatment.

The human mind is powerful and can influence life greatly. This is why it is important to have a positive attitude about everything, including illness.

The following variable should also be considered, although some of you may have a hard time accepting it. As written in the book of Ecclesiastes, there is a time to live and a time to die. This is very true. There is a juncture in a person's life where the time to leave the living has arrived. Despite this fact, many people fight this and try to cheat death at any cost. An initiated or enlightened person recognizes the divine order associated with life and death. An acceptance of physical death as a transition to the heavenly fields is a knowing that becomes inherent in a spiritually and psychically advanced human being.

In other circumstances, energy healing can calm a person's soul and give peace of mind. Some may attain a spiritual awakening just prior to death. This can happen whether or not an individual heals from an affliction.

Emotions can be healed and a deep spirituality attained through energy work. Essentially, you can heal yourself or help others heal themselves on a physical, emotional or spiritual level by employing these high vibrations of energy.

The Characteristics of Healing Colors

You will now be taught methods to use healing colors in your sessions or treatments.

The colors of a rainbow seen in the sky after a rainstorm are similar in color and beauty to the healing colors that come down from the heavenly fields, though healing colors contain much higher vibratory rates than the rainbow colors. These wonderful healing colors have different vibratory rates or frequencies. We will discuss all of these special energies beginning in order from lowest vibration to highest vibration.

Red

Although all the healing colors vibrate at an extremely high rate or frequency, the color red has the lowest vibration of all of these. This lumination should be considered as a hot energy or very warm energy. Many people that work with this color will experience or sense some heat or warmth as it flows into the chakras and body. This healing color is perceived as a deep and luxurious red hue. It is used for increasing stamina and vitality within. Clients or patients that suffer from circulatory problems and arthritis may benefit somewhat from the application of this color. However, it can alleviate conditions and discomfort but can not truly be used to heal serious conditions.

Orange

This healing color vibrates at a slightly higher rate than red. Its temperature is in a very warm to medium warm range. If you can picture the orange in a rainbow or the light spectrum, then you can realize what this orange healing color looks like. When this color flows into the crown chakra and down into the rest of the chakras and body, it will be felt or sensed as a very pleasant warm sensation. This particular healing color is important for fighting inflammation, sores, and body stiffness. It is particularly useful in creating a sense of well-being within. As in the case of the color red, this healing color can not be used to heal major diseases and illnesses. It has a temporary, short-term effect on a person.

Yellow

The healing color yellow vibrates at mid-range between the lowest and highest healing colors. Existing at a higher vibratory rate than the orange color, this lumination has a greater healing potential. It has a pretty light-yellow hue similar to a yellow tulip or sunshine. This healing color can be felt or sensed as a slightly warm sensation. It is particularly beneficial in the treatment of infections, colds, and in the general cleansing of the lymphatic system. Therefore, it helps to restore balance to the immune system. Also, it aids in the healing of circulatory problems. It has a more long-term affect upon the human body, aura, and chakras than the orange healing energy. However, yellow healing color does not truly heal on a permanent basis.

Green

This healing color has a high vibratory rate and is considered a true healing energy. This green lumination is similar to the light-green color of new leaves in springtime. It is a powerful healing color that can be used for all types of healing. It is very beneficial in the treatment of cancer, arthritis, some painful afflictions, disorders of the immune system, and general illnesses. Gifted healers draw in this high vibration of healing energy. It is felt as a lukewarm to slightly cool sensation by patients experiencing this healing energy. If used a few times during energy work, this special healing color has a long-term, if not permanent, healing potential.

Light Blue

The light-blue healing color has a very high frequency or rate of vibration. Although gentler, this blue color is more powerful than the green healing color. It is similar in appearance to the light blue of the sky on a summer day. This healing lumination is felt or sensed as a soothing, cool sensation. If you can imagine cool water flowing over your skin gently, then you can get an understanding of what it feels like. As a true and powerful healing color, light blue is beneficial for the treatment of all diseases and disorders including cancer. It is particularly beneficial in balancing the endocrine glandular system. Also, it has a soothing effect on the body and emotions. The light-blue color has a prolonged, if not permanent effect on the body, soul, aura, and chakras. Initiated or spiritually enlightened people use this wonderful healing color.

Indigo or Mid-Blue

The indigo or mid-blue healing color vibrates at an extremely high rate or frequency. Although it is at a higher vibration than the special healing colors of light blue and green, it is not used normally as a healing color for diseases. It is associated more with the enhancement of mind power, and to a lesser degree with psychic ability expansion. This high vibration of color helps with mental acuity and clearing of the mind. It allows the brain, directed by the mind, to connect with the Universal Consciousness or Divine Mind above. On a physical level, the indigo or mid-blue healing color affects the nerves, cells and muscles of the body in a very positive manner. When this color is employed during energy work, it sends rejuvenating energy to these parts of the human body. This color is experienced as a very cool sensation. Aura readers and medical intuitives can perceive it as a rich blue similar to the color of the ocean.

Violet or Light Purple

The healing color of violet or light purple is at an even higher frequency or vibration than mid-blue. As a true healing color it has the ability to heal the human soul rather than the physical body. It should be remembered that healing affects the mind, body and soul. This is the special color that vibrates and harmonizes with the eternal soul within. For those who experience this color, it is felt as a very cool sensation. The actual hue or tint of this healing lumination ranges from a mid-purple to a light purple. People with the ability to see auras and higher vibrations of energy perceive it as a color similar to a beautiful purple light found in sunsets. It is a powerful energy that can send tingling sensations all over the head of the person working with it. It allows a deep spirituality to develop within an individual. In some cases, this can be extremely important for a person that is dying. In essence, the soul becomes healed. It allows someone to pass over to the other side with the knowledge that there is something better than the earthly realm.

Gold

The gold color has a rate of vibration slightly higher than the violet or light-purple healing color. The light spectrum and the colors of the rainbow were used as examples of what the healing colors look like. The gold is an additional color that exists in the heavenly fields. It can also come down from this realm into the crown chakra and aura of a person. This occurs when a person opens up more in a psychic and spiritual way. This lumination helps people attain enlightenment and leads to a deeper understanding of the mysteries of life. Also, it is highly beneficial in cleansing the human aura and the chakra system. A person working with this healing color will sense or feel it as either warm or cool energy flowing over the head and sometimes through the body. Essentially, a person's auric field will become brighter, cleaner, and more expanded after this. This healing energy will work through the chakras and into the nervous system and tissues of the body. This raises the vibrations of the cells, tissues and organs of the physical form. This helps protect a person from developing diseases within.

White

The white healing color is unique and has the highest vibration or frequency of all the healing colors. It is actually a Divine Light sometimes referred to as the Light of God. All seven colors, and the gold color are contained within the white light. These colors radiate outwards from this powerful healing color to become their own healing essences. The white light will flow down from the heavens above, into the crown chakra and into the aura, chakras, and body in many instances. When this occurs, the other healing colors working on their own will still flow into the crown energy center. An aura reader will see this color as a very bright white light. This divine lumination is beneficial for all types of physical, emotional, and spiritual healing. It is the only healing color capable of healing the mind, body, and soul. Someone experiencing this white color will feel or sense a combination of warm and cool sensations in any or all parts of the body. It has the ability to clean, brighten, and expand the human energy field or aura. This is the special healing color that the Master Teacher Jesus used during his ministry.

As an initiated or enlightened person, you can learn to work with these healing colors. As you open your chakras up and develop the power of the mind, the ability to see, sense and use these high vibrations of energy becomes evident.

True teachers, healers, and counselors use some or all of these colors either on a conscious or subconscious level.

The Final Initiation, along with many of the techniques and exercises in this book, are designed to help you to achieve this goal.

The Candle Flame and Colors Exercise

The Candle Flame and Colors Exercise will be covered in detail. Begin by placing either a white candle or light-colored candle in its holder on a top of a flat surface. (Do not use a dark-colored candle because dark-colored candles have a slightly different vibration of energy that can sometimes interfere with desired results.)

Make sure that the room is very dark. Eliminate any light sources as this can also interfere with the results of the exercise. Once you have done this, light the candle. Then sit down in a comfortable position about five feet away from the lighted candle in the candleholder. Take in a deep breath and hold it for a few seconds. Release it slowly and evenly out the nose. Repeat the process two more times and then return to normal breathing. Begin to gaze at the lighted candle. Stare directly into the flame for a few seconds. As you do, pay attention to the various colors that you start to see within the candle flame. You may see white, blue, red, or even yellow colors as you gaze into the flame. After the few seconds are up, move your gaze just slightly to the right side of the flame. Then let your eyes move to the edge or perimeter of the flame.

Area to focus on and visualize specific colors—red, orange, yellow, green, light blue, indigo, purple, and white. Each color to be concentrated on in respective order (aura or corona area is the focal point).

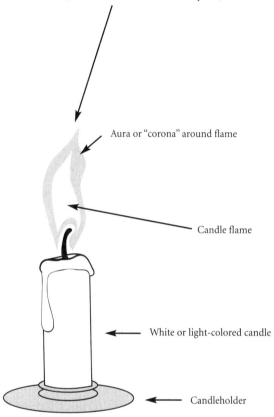

Aura or "corona" around flame

Candle flame

White or light-colored candle

Candleholder

Figure 8.1: Candle Flame and Colors Exercise.

Start to stare at this point just on the right edge of the flame for a while. As you focus on this spot think of all of the healing colors. Begin with the colors of the lowest vibrations and work your way up. In other words, think of the color red for a second. Imagine or visualize this color in your mind. Then, think of the color orange and see or imagine this color for a brief moment. Next, concentrate on the color yellow in the same manner. Continue this by focusing on the green, the light blue, the indigo or mid-blue, and finally the violet or light purple in the same way.

After focusing on all seven healing colors, do the same thing with the gold and white colors. Once you have thought about and visualized each and every color in your mind, you can move on to the next part of the exercise.

Now you will repeat the same exercise but in a slightly different manner. This time as you think of the color red, imagine the red starting to materialize on the perimeter of the candle flame. Keep staring at the right hand edge for several seconds. During this time, you may actually start to see a slightly red tinge about the perimeter of the flame, especially on the right hand side that you are concentrating on. If you do not see any noticeable change while doing this gazing exercise, simply relax and continue with the Candle Flame and Colors Exercise. This technique is training your mind and will eventually work for you as you practice a few more times. After several seconds, let your gaze move all around the edge of the flame. Simply direct your eyes from the right side upward to the very top of the candle flame's edge or perimeter. From here, allow the eyes to move downward to the left side of the flame's perimeter. Essentially, you will be sweeping the whole edge of the candle flame with your eyes. Of course, this will be done from right to left.

Repeat the same process with the color orange. After that, try the healing color yellow. Then continue with the following healing colors green, light blue, indigo or mid-blue, violet, or light purple.

Upon completing this part of the focusing exercise using the seven main healing colors, try it with the healing color gold and finally the white light or color.

A certain fact needs to be stated. As you succeed in seeing these various healing colors appear before your eyes, do not think that it is your imagination. When you develop your psychic and spiritual abilities, you also develop other powers associated with the human mind. You are actually changing the vibrations of the candle flame and manifesting these colors. This is the power of concentration and mind projection.

Once you have focused on the final healing color white, take your eyes away from the candle. Let the eyes return to normal sight. If you need to, gaze about the room for a moment or two until you feel that you have returned to a normal state of consciousness. Concentrating on your breathing for a few seconds may also help. Afterwards, distinguish the candle flame, preferably with a candle snuffer. Return to your regular business. You should be comfortable in knowing that this exercise is still working on a subtle level inside your brain.

The Candle Flame and Colors Exercise can be attempted several more times in the future, if you wish. Eventually, your ability to see higher energies such as healing colors, auras and chakras will increase. As this happens, you will no longer need to use this exercise. For the moment though, it is a positive step to increase some of your psychic ability. This ability can be taken one step further. It involves working with healing colors on your clients, patients, and friends.

Visualizing Colors and Projection Exercise

When you feel that you have become adept at visualizing and projecting colors around the aura or perimeter of the candle flame, you can proceed to the next step. You can use the same process described in the Candle Flame and Colors Exercise on a client or patient. Simply, have the person sit comfortably in a chair directly in front of you. Make sure that she has a white or light-colored wall behind her head as a background. The room should have an appearance of a near dusk environment. These two preparations will allow you to see her auric field in an easier manner.

Next, do a few deep breathing exercises and then return to normal breathing. As you do this start gazing above or around her head. Allow your eyes to become slightly out of focus. Let your gaze stare beyond the top or side of the head. The eyes should stare through the wall for a few moments. You should start to see the aura about the client's head. At this point bring your focus back to above and around the head. You are now looking at the aura around the crown chakra.

Some of you may see a white light around the head about two to three inches out from the surface. Many of you will see some colors such as yellow or blue. For some of you who are aura readers, you will see or sense various colors of the aura or energy field. In any case, remain gazing at her crown energy center and area. It is an easy technique to use. The more you practice the easier it becomes to see and sense the human energy field.

Now, as you continue to gaze at the subject's aura, repeat the same procedure that you tried in the Candle Flame and Colors Exercise. Start with the color red and work through all of these healing colors until you have finished up with the white light.

In the previous exercise, the candle represented the person's head, the flame represented the aura, and the perimeter of the flame represented the edge or perimeter of the aura.

Once you have tried this procedure on your client, friend, or patient, simply let your eyes return to normal vision. You may need to blink a few times in order to get your eyes and your mind back to normal.

Everyone is different and will experience different results the first time that the Visualizing Colors and Projection Exercise is attempted. Some of you who see auras easily will probably have success in seeing some or all of these healing colors manifesting about the client's head. If you do, the colors will be seen around both the edges of the aura and into the crown chakra. It may even appear as colors flowing downward into the crown energy center and over the face.

For others, little or no change in the person's auric field will be seen or sensed. This is nothing to be concerned about. If you continue to practice on a regular basis, success will come. Many of you may see or sense some colors. This is good sign that you are opening up more of your abilities to see and work with higher vibrations of energy. In any event, the key is to practice this technique until you become very comfortable with it. You can add this procedure into your own healing modalities.

As you see and sense the human aura more easily, the healing colors begin to appear soon afterward while working with clients or patients. Eventually, this will happen whether or not you focus on any or all of these illuminations. This is part of the advancement of your gifts.

As your own vibrations become higher and your auric field stronger, these healing colors will come automatically while you work with a client. The next event that occurs is a change of the colors manifesting on top of your client or subject's head.

Soon the illuminations having the lowest vibratory rate stop manifesting in your client's crown chakra and energy field. The healing colors yellow, green, light blue, and white start to appear on a regular basis as you work with each and every subject or client. These become the predominant healing colors that flow into your client's chakras, aura, and body. This is because your own healing abilities have increased. You are now working with much higher vibrations of healing energy. Either consciously or subconsciously, you are able to draw in these important healing colors. In essence, you have increased the vibrations within yourself and your healing room.

Occasionally, the high vibrations of mid-blue or indigo, violet, or light purple and gold, will manifest about your subject's crown energy center and aura. This sometimes occurs for the following reasons:

- Firstly, if you or your client knows that a specific type of healing color is necessary, then the appropriate lumination will manifest. Once again, this can happen on a conscious or subconscious level.

- Secondly, there is a supreme intelligence present in everything on earth and in the heavens above. This intelligence sometimes referred to as the Divine Mind, Divine Intelligence, or Universal Mind determines the appropriate healing energy or colors that are needed for your patient or client.

- Thirdly, your client's higher self that is connected with the Divine Mind allows this healing process to unfold.

Many people confuse the healing colors that come down from the heavenly fields with the colors of the human aura and the chakras. Although these colors all appear as similar in regards to hue and tint, the vibratory rates or frequencies are all different.

The healing colors red, orange, yellow, green, light blue, mid-blue or indigo, violet or light purple, gold, and white have the highest vibrations. The colors of the human aura or energy field have a slightly lower vibration than these colors.

The colors associated with the seven major chakras of the human chakra system have slightly lower vibrations than the aura. Of course, these chakra colors, from lowest to highest vibration, are red, orange, yellow, green, blue, indigo, and purple. These colors are located in the base, the sacral, the solar plexus, the heart, the throat, the third eye, and the crown chakras, respectively.

Although the aura colors and the chakra colors exist at lower vibratory rates or frequencies than the healing colors, all of these colors still possess extremely high rates of vibrations. These colors all work in harmony with each other, as well.

As you use the energy techniques mentioned in the last chapter on your client, the healing colors flow into the crown energy center, into the aura and into all the major chakras. As these colors mix with the colors of the auric field, any negative or dirty illuminations are removed. They are replaced with beautiful healing colors that lower their frequencies and harmonize with the aura.

Also, these healing colors, especially yellow, green, light blue, and white, will join with each consecutive chakra. To an aura reader, these energies will appear as a swirl or mist of pretty colors intermingling with the particular chakra or energy center. Think of each chakra as a swirl or wheel of colored light. Then, add in the dancing colors of the Northern Lights. This should give you a general idea what this looks like.

The healing illuminations step down their frequencies in order to harmonize with the chakra colors. These special colors seem to have a mind of their own as they flow into and through each major chakra. Essentially, the healing energies will go where they are needed.

The healing colors and Universal Energy will flow into the nervous system, the lymphatic system, the circulatory system, the organs, and the cells of the body. This is accomplished when these healing essences lower their respective vibratory rates in order to assimilate with the human form.

The more you practice these techniques, the more you develop a true potential to move and direct healing energies through others. This is a goal that all true healers should strive toward.

In this chapter, two of the four elements were used. These were air and fire; air being the breath, fire being the candle flame. This should give you more of an understanding of how important the four elements are in spiritualism and healing.

As a truly initiated and enlightened person you recognize that you do not heal anyone. It is the Creator, the Great Spirit, God, or the Supreme Intelligence that heals. Along with this, a person needing healing allows his or her own healing energy within to work in partnership with this Supreme presence. You are merely a channel or instrument in all of this. Please, keep a humble mind when you develop your healing attributes.

"Earth has no sorrow that Heaven can not heal."

—Thomas Moore

Chapter 9

Soul Travel Training and Soul Healing Techniques

"Man, tree, and flower are supposed to die; but the fact remains that God's universe is spiritual and immortal . . ."

—Mary Baker Eddy

The human soul is eternal and linked to God, the Creator, or Great Spirit. A person on a spiritual path knows this and understands that they are a soul with a body and not a body with a soul. The human mind that controls the physical brain is closely associated with the soul. In fact, the mind can be considered part of the soul. It is responsible for your awareness or consciousness of your surroundings.

Soul travel or astral travel is a unique and marvelous experience that allows you to travel anywhere. Some of the places you can visit exist in either the physical earthly realm or the heavenly realm. As a soul traveler you can go to other countries of the world, visit the homes of friends and loved ones, explore many ancient sites, and even browse about your own neighborhood.

Soul travel can also take you to healing temples, teaching temples, crystal palaces, and beautiful gardens that exist in heaven. You can even visit the Akashic Records or Universal Library. This is a magical place where all knowledge, wisdom, and information are stored. It is located on a higher field or plane of the heavenly fields.

It is here that you can access information about any or all of your past lives. This happens when you review your own soul records. These records can be thought of as an ancient book or scroll that contains all of your past, present, and future history. This is a very quick and proficient way of delving into your previous lifetimes. As well, it shows you a glimpse of possible future events in this lifetime.

Everyone soul travels while sleeping. Many people recall these events as lucid dreams or "flying dreams." They will feel very real to the person. When you fall asleep the Law of Magnetism takes over. Your body enters into a very relaxed mode and your brain wave patterns slow down dramatically. This changes the magnetic polarity of the human body. Normally, the body has a more negative charge or polarity but becomes more positive at this time.

On the other hand, the human soul has a more positive polarity. As the brain wave patterns alter, the mind becomes free to direct or influence the soul. Both mind and soul have a natural inclination to leave the body at this moment. Under the Law of Magnetism positive and negative charges attract while positive and positive repel. This is the same situation in regard to the soul and body. The more positively charged soul, and the body, which has become more positive, start to push or repel each other. This makes it easier for the human soul to slip out of the physical form.

Unfortunately, most people most of the time do not remember their soul travel dreams whether these are in the form of flying dreams or lucid dreams. There are methods available to recall soul travel during sleep. Also, these same methods can be used to train you or your clients to soul travel in a waking but altered state of consciousness. You can even train yourself to soul or astral travel in a near sleeping state, too.

Preparations for Soul Travel Training

Prior to attempting soul travel, certain preparations are important in order to give you a better chance of success. These preparations involve diet, breathing, and water.

Diet

Diet can influence soul travel in many situations. This is especially true regarding soul travel in waking or light sleep states. Once again, the Law of Magnetism comes into play. As in the case of the human soul and body, most foods have either a more positive essence or a more negative essence. Ultimately, the consumption of these foods whether positively oriented or negatively oriented, can affect the body's polarity.

It was mentioned earlier that the body contains both positive and negative polarities. For a moment, picture the human body as similar to a car battery. The battery contains both electrons and protons; the electrons being negative and the protons being positive. Both these essences are necessary for the flow of electricity and the smooth operation of the battery.

The physical body requires both the positive and negative essences to work in a healthy and harmonious nature. Although the body contains both polarities it is still more negatively charged. This is also true with certain foods. They can be either more negative or more positive.

Some foods that have a more positive essence are green leafy vegetables, some seeds such as sesame seeds, and many fruits. In particular, kiwi fruit, mangoes, apples, cherries, and citrus fruits have a more positive essence and less negative essence. These foods should be considered as having a lighter or higher vibratory rate. They are sometimes referred to as "spirit food" due to the high frequency and the more positive essence that they contain.

Many foods such as red meats, pork, pastries, ice cream, and sweet snacks possess a more negative essence and a less positive essence. These foods should be considered as having a heavier or lower vibratory rate.

Some foods such as chicken, other poultry products, fish, seafood, and most dairy products have an equal balance of positive and negative essences or polarities. These can be considered as neutral foods and have vibratory rates somewhere between the spirit foods and the heavier foods.

Breathing

The breath of life is very important for soul travel training. In chapter 3, the benefits associated with deep breathing were explained. Feel free to review this information if you wish.

When you draw in breath you bring in the chi or Universal Energy. If you hold this breath of life in your lungs for a few seconds, then this energy will flow via the circulatory system to the entire body. Of course, this raises your vibrations and allows your physical body to become lighter and of a more positive essence. Therefore, deep breathing has a somewhat similar effect as spirit food on the body.

Deep breathing exercises can be taken one step further when attempting soul or astral travel. This involves taking in deep breaths and holding the air in your lungs for a period longer than five seconds. The longer the breath is held, the more positively charged the body becomes. Also, the vibrations of the body become much higher. Obviously, the breath can only be held for a time that is not too difficult or uncomfortable.

Water

Water can have a twofold effect on the body when used in a certain way. Anyone seriously considering soul travel should drink proper amounts of water during the day. This has a tendency to flush the body and remove unwanted wastes, poisons and byproducts that have a very low vibratory rate. The cleansing of these undesireable substances helps the physical form to maintain healthy energy within.

In *Ancient Teachings for Beginners,* the Glass of Water Technique was described. This technique teaches you how to magnetize or "charge" water in a glass, thereby giving it a higher vibration of energy. This has great potential when used in soul travel training.

The combination of spirit foods, extended deep breathing exercises, and the magnetizing or charging of water can all be used together in the following manner. This will ensure that you have a better chance of success when attempting soul travel.

For seven days prior to attempting any soul travel techniques, the following regimen should be tried. A week is normally the required time necessary for the desired energy changes in the body and the soul to manifest. During this period, your diet should be looked at closely. If you are a vegetarian and do not have a sweet tooth then the chances are you will not have to adjust your diet. On the other hand, if you have substantial amounts of red meat in your diet, then you should try to limit the amount of red meat during this short duration of time. Also, if you love sweets, you should try to cut back on these delicacies for the seven days.

Bear in mind that this is only a temporary situation and these guidelines are not written in stone. Try to find a happy balance that works for you. In any case, soul travel can be attained whether you are a meat eater or a strict vegetarian. It is simply easier to learn to soul travel if you can make these changes during the preparation stage. If you are adept at soul travel then these preparations may increase the soul travel or out-of-body experiences that you have.

Green leafy vegetables have some of the highest vibratory rates of all of the spirit foods. They possess an abundance of positive essence. This is especially true of lettuce and spinach. If you can eat large amounts of these two vegetables over the seven days, the benefits may be felt during soul travel attempts.

You can also practice longer deep breathing exercises during the preparation stage. The deep breathing should be done twice a day, in the morning and then again in the evening prior to sleep. If you do shift work and have a different schedule, then feel free to adjust this accordingly.

Begin each morning by taking a deep breath into the lungs. Then, as you hold it, count to twelve slowly in your mind. As you do this feel the lungs as they start to pulse. You will begin to feel pressure in the chest. When you reach ten it is time to let the breath out. Release the breath slowly through your mouth. Avoid the urge to rush it out. Expel all your air. Then repeat the exercise in the same manner. Do the same deep breathing a third and final time that morning. Return to normal breathing and return to your everyday activities. In the evening, do the deep breathing exercise three times in the exact same way that you did in the morning. Follow the same deep breathing regimen for six more days.

You may start to notice that your body feels as if it is vibrating or moving back in forth. This is a normal occurrence. Your body is becoming more positive allowing your eternal soul to begin slipping out. Your soul is moving slightly out of the physical and into the auric field and then it moves back within.

During the week, the Glass of Water Technique should be practiced once every day or at least once every other day. In any case, try to do this following technique a minimum of three times over this period of preparation.

First of all, fill an average glass with water and then find a relatively quiet place to sit. Place the full glass of water down beside you. Next do the Fire-and-Hand-Warming Technique described in chapter 5. Review this technique, if needed. After this, pick the glass of water up. Place your hands in a comfortable position around the glass making sure that you maintain contact with the surface. This will ensure that the healing energy and chi flows into the water where it is absorbed.

Remember that the right hand possesses the positive essence of this chi or Universal Energy while the left hand has the negative essence of this energy. It was mentioned that under the Law of Magnetism, like repels like and like attracts unlike. Therefore the positive essence of the right hand attracts the negative essence of the left hand. This results in these two essences combining as one in the water. Eventually, the water will become magnetized or charged and have a higher vibratory rate. The positive polarity will be the dominant essence contained within the water.

Now, feel the warmth and energy moving through the wrists and into the hands. Concentrate on this for a few moments until you feel a warm, pulsing sensation in the hands, thumbs, and fingers. Let this pulsing get stronger.

Allow your focus to move to the glass of water. Sense the hands pulsing against the surface of the glass. Feel this pulsing getting stronger and stronger until it feels like a throbbing or beating "heart" emanating from the glass of water. The water will begin to feel different to you. Continue to hold the glass for about five minutes. It may feel as if the glass is trying to push your hands away from it. The water has now been fully magnetized. The chi or healing energy existing within the water is sometimes referred to as vital life force.

Take the glass of water and drink it down quickly. Soon, you might start to feel a pleasant warm sensation in the tummy. This is a sign that the charged water is having a positive effect upon the body. The vibratory rate of the body has been raised and contains more of a positive essence within.

By the end of the seven day period of preparation, the combination of diet, deep breathing, and water will give you the necessary changes to your vibratory rate to allow you to soul travel. You are now ready to begin.

Basic Soul Travel Technique

On the eighth day you can attempt the following technique. This exercise can be used on a regular basis. It is simple and easy.

Make sure that you are relaxed. All negative emotions such as anger or fear should be put aside. The room should be fairly quiet. Sit down in a comfortable chair with a full glass of water placed nearby. Take in one deep breath, hold it for a few moments and then release it slowly through the nose. Repeat this a second and third time. Return to normal breathing.

Pick up the glass and do the Glass of Water Technique again. This time you might notice an improvement while performing this technique. Your hands may begin to pulse faster and stronger than previous attempts. As before, drink down all of the charged water.

From this point, you can either stay in the chair or lie down in a comfortable position. This is entirely up to you. However, if you practice this technique just prior to bedtime, then the latter position would probably be the best one. For simplicity's sake, a bed will be used during the instructions.

As you lie here visualize or imagine a white light encircling the inside of the walls of your bedroom. Then, visualize another white light completely encircling you and your bed. Basically, you will have an inner and an outer circle of white light surrounding you while you attempt to astral or soul travel. This is a measure of protection that helps to keep negative entities and spirits from bothering you. These white lights also attract angels, spirit guides, and other heavenly beings toward you.

As an initiated and enlightened person your strong aura and higher vibrations will help to draw the proper and loving spirit beings toward you. The energy work and spiritual awakening has brought you to this moment in your life. Of course, you should always ask for your angels and spirit guides to enter the room during meditation or soul travel. This request ensures that these beings of light come to protect and work with you. Although angels, spirit guides, and others are different in some ways, they all work together in harmony. These spirit beings are all part of the hierarchy of the heavenly fields.

By this time, you may be feeling some warmth in the pit of your stomach. You might also experience the sensation that your body is vibrating either side-to-side or back and forth. This is the result of the magnetized water and indicates that your soul is trying to slip out.

Now the longer deep breathing techniques will be used. You can think of these as breath holding techniques, too. In this circumstance, you will do the longer deep breathing or breath holding techniques twice in the same manner as before. The third deep breath will be done differently. After releasing all of your breath the second time, wait for about three or four seconds. Let your eyes look toward the foot of the bed and imagine that you are standing here looking back at your prone body. Shut your eyes and picture this in your mind.

Now take in the third breath and hold it for the slow count of twelve. Then, release your breath in a forceful fashion. Expel all of your breath quickly. As you do this feel as if you are pushing yourself out of the physical body. At this point, let yourself relax. Everyone will have different results when attempting this part of the technique. A few of you might slip out of the body and end up at the foot of your bed staring back at your reclining form. Some of you may notice very little result when you try this the first few times. However, most of you will have some positive results. For instance, you may feel as if you are vibrating within your body in a very powerful way. Perhaps you might be aware of moving out of the body a few feet for a second or two. You may even feel pleasant sensations throughout and some light-headedness.

The secret to successful soul travel is to keep practicing this technique on a regular basis until you become more adept. Eventually, many of you will be able to consciously astral travel. This can be in a light altered state or in a near sleep state.

An additional step should be done whether you are attempting this while in a sitting position or just prior to falling asleep. Afterward either say to yourself or mumble the following affirmation, *"I want to soul travel. I want to visit the Akashic Records."* If you wish to travel to other places such as healing temples or teaching temples, simply substitute the words "Akashic Records" with either or both temple names. This same approach can be used if you wish to visit a friend on the earthly realm or to visit crystal rooms and palaces in the heavenly realm.

If you use this affirmation prior to sleep, this thought will enter into the subconsciousness and the mind of your soul. This conditions or programs you to eventually sojourn to these desired destinations. After saying or thinking these words just drift off to sleep.

If you are doing the soul travel technique while sitting in a comfortable chair, use the same affirmation. Then daydream for a moment or two. After that, arise from your sitting position and return to your normal activities. Know that the affirmation will work through the same process as falling asleep.

When you soul or astral travel you can meet and work with angels, spirit guides, and other light beings. These members of the heavenly hierarchy will accompany you to many marvelous places. Some, such as healers and teachers, will be waiting for you in the healing temples and teaching temples of the heavenly fields. You can learn to communicate with all of these wise beings of light. Answers you need, knowledge and wisdom you seek, can be obtained from these beings. You might even find peace of mind and contentment while visiting a beautiful garden in heaven. This can be a healing and soothing experience for many of you.

Advanced Soul Travel Technique

In the last chapter several energy flow techniques were explained to you. Two of these techniques can be combined together and employed for the express purpose of soul travel. These are the Crown-to-Base Chakra Energy Flow Technique and the Water Fountain and Feet Chakra Technique. Essentially, the combination of both of these into one longer and complete technique allows the energy to flow through the entire body. This exercise is called the Chakra Flow Induction Technique. The word "induction" refers to the ability to induce the proper altered state of consciousness needed for past-life regression and soul travel.

Initially you should use the Chakra Flow Induction Technique on yourself. Practice the technique until you are very adept at it. It may become second nature for some of you who are natural energy feelers. Eventually, this technique can be attempted on clients or subjects if you wish.

This time begin by focusing on the crown energy center. Move the energy down to the base and back up again. Repeat this energy flow three to four times, allowing it to flow faster and faster. Remember to think of this energy as warm water. Next, move the warm flow of energy or water down to the feet. Visualize the warm water rushing up your feet to the crown.

Then, direct the energy back down your body, from the crown to the feet. Focus on this warm water or energy moving even faster, up and down the body. Allow this energy to become stronger and more powerful so that it will flow on its own. As this happens, visualize your angel or spirit guide meeting you. Imagine your angel or guide holding your hand and floating upward with you, taking you to a place you desire to visit. This can be a healing temple, a teaching temple, the Akashic Records, or anywhere else you would like to visit. Let your mind drift allowing any images or visions to enter. Enjoy this for as long as you want.

When you feel that your mind has drifted long enough, focus on your body once more. Feel the energy sensations flowing through your chakras and physical form. As you do this concentrate on the warm water starting to slow down.

Keep focusing on this energy, making it slow down even more. Finally, stop the energy in either the heart or crown chakra. This is up to you. After this, just relax for a few moments and let your mind return to normal consciousness. When you are ready go about your regular business. Try the Advanced Soul Travel Technique as often as you wish.

By doing the basic and advanced soul travel techniques you will become more experienced with soul travel. For those of you who already soul travel easily, these exercises will help you to visit more varied and marvelous places.

Soul Healing

Eventually, you can develop the ability to do healing while you are in your soul form. Gifted and enlightened healers such as the Master Jesus were accomplished at this. This ability allows you the healer to travel anywhere or any distance quickly in order to do your healing work on a person.

Oftentimes, healing angels and other healing beings will travel with you while you are in your soul form. As a team you will enter into the home, bedroom, or hospital room of the person needing healing work. If the individual is willing and her higher self wishes it, then you along with your healing helpers will be allowed to work on her. You can place your "soul hands" upon the person in order to send healing energy to the afflicted area. A healing angel or two will do the same thing. In your soul essence, you can also move your soul hands into the body to work on specific areas requiring attention. As well, any healers with you will do the same type of procedure.

This powerful method of healing normally transpires under the following conditions:

You must be in either a deep, altered state or asleep.

The client or patient must be in a relaxed and receptive state or asleep.

Prior to sleep you should focus on the person and the person's name. Say in your mind that you want to do healing work on this person and then ask for healing angels and guides to help you. Following that let yourself go to sleep.

The next day you may or may not be aware of the results of your attempt. Your intuition might help in this situation. You might feel that something has happened. Perhaps you will remember a dream in which you laid your hands upon the person and sensed or saw beings of light near you. In any case, there is a very good chance that the procedure was successful.

Sometimes, the person receiving the healing will remember your visitation. This can be in the form of a vivid dream. The individual may also see or sense a person or a presence in the room during the night. These are indications that you soul traveled there. In some situations, an emotional healing not a physical healing may be the result. The more your practice soul healing, the better you become at it.

Distance, Absent, and Remote Healing

Once you develop or enhance your gifts of energy healing and soul travel, you can increase another ability. This is the ability to send healing energy to someone or something at a distance. This ability can be accomplished through a certain technique. This technique is referred to as distance healing, absent healing, or remote healing. Distance healing is the most commonly used phrase for this method of energy healing.

Many schools of discipline use different symbols when they teach their variations of this healing method. Symbols are important because they train you to focus your own healing energy.

In ancient times, the healing temples and mystery schools of Egypt employed four specific symbols for distance healing.

These symbols are the Ankh, the Solar Winged Disc, the Sun, and the Eye of Horus:

- The *Ankh* represents the symbol for life and is used for healing of cancer.
- The *Solar Winged Disc* symbol is used for emotional healing.
- The *Sun* is representative of vitality and is used for the healing of most other diseases.
- The *Eye of Horus* is used for spiritual healing and enlightenment.

These were secret symbols taught only to a few of the more advanced or initiated students of the mystery schools and healing temples. As in ancient times these symbols are still powerful and can be used today.

When performing a distance healing treatment on someone you can employ these symbols in the following manner.

The Ankh symbol—used for healing cancer

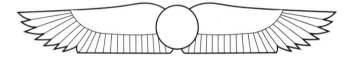

The Solar Winged Disc symbol—
used for emotional healing

The Eye of Horus symbol—
used for spiritual healing and enlightenment

Figure 9.1: The four special Egyptian symbols used in distance or absent healing.

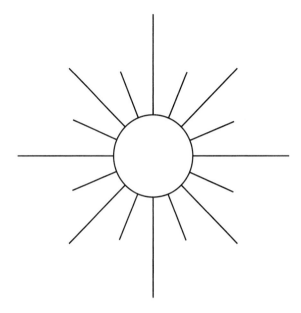

The Sun symbol—used for healing most other diseases

Find a quiet place and make sure that you remove any distractions. Get yourself into a comfortable position. Lying or sitting in bed is an ideal position. If this treatment is attempted just prior to sleep, then so much the better.

Do some deep breathing for a few moments. This should help you to relax. When ready, picture or imagine in your mind the person who needs healing. Mention the subject's name in your head and not out loud. Focus on this client or subject for a brief moment. Choose the healing symbol that best represents this person. For instance, if the client has cancer use the Ankh symbol and so forth. Next, see the symbol in your mind and send it to her. Send thoughts of love to the individual as well. Completely release these thoughts and try to dismiss them from your mind. Finally, think about something else or let your mind drift. Soon, you may fall asleep. This helps the healing energy to be released thereby sending it to the afflicted person.

As you become stronger and more proficient at doing distance healing, you will not need to use the symbols. Ultimately, your focusing of energy followed by its release will be all that is required. The use of symbols is for the purpose of training and can be eliminated from your procedure when you feel you are ready.

In this chapter three of the four elements were used. These were air, water, and earth. The breath represented the air, warm water as energy represented the water, and the Water Fountain and Feet Chakra Technique represented both water and earth. By drawing energy up from the feet you also draw in the energy of the earth.

As a human you are a multidimensional being. You can operate in both the earthly and the heavenly realms if you choose to do so. As a human soul you are a light being and a spark of the Creator or Great Spirit. As an enlightened or initiated one, you can use your potential gifts to help manifest Heaven on Earth.

"May you receive all the spiritual blessings of life."

—Douglas De Long

Chapter 10

Hypatia and the Alexandrian Library

"There is only one good—knowledge, and one evil—ignorance."

—Socrates

All the techniques described in *Ancient Healing Techniques* were designed to help you develop or enhance your abilities. If you are already working as an energy healer, hopefully some chapters in the book have helped you to increase your healing gifts. For those of you who are counselors or teachers, the step-by-step instructions have allowed you to become more gifted in your chosen fields.

Detailed instructions were given to you for soul travel and past-life recall. If you are not already experienced with these two forms of spiritual exploration, do not worry. By practicing many of the exercises contained in this book, you will become more adept at soul or astral traveling and recalling previous incarnations.

When you become proficient at soul travel, you can visit the Akashic Records or Universal Library when needed. It is here in this section of the heavenly fields that time stands still. All the events, knowledge and wisdom of the past, present, and even the future, exist here.

By visiting certain areas of the Akashic Records, you can access incredible amounts of information. If you can think of time as a river that flows endlessly, with no beginning or end, then you can gain an understanding of our true existence.

Everything that has ever happened and will happen is stored here in this amazing Universal Library. Learn to view historical events from earlier times. Answers to questions that you may have can be found here.

Not only can you view events of the past but also your own previous incarnations. This can be done while you are asleep or in an altered state of consciousness.

It was also mentioned that future events are stored in the Universal Library. As an advanced soul traveler, you can see into your own future. When you envision yourself a year or two from now doing something you love and appearing happy, a great comfort or peace settles within your being. This can give you a certain knowing inside that you are on the right path and that all is unfolding as it should.

The author has the ability to explore the Akashic Records in order to learn about events of the past. This is done while he is either in a sleep state or in a deeply altered state of consciousness. The following story that you are about to read was received in this manner.

The Christian Church had suffered through ten horrible persecutions stretching over many years. The last one had been at the time of Emperor Diocletian.

All this changed abruptly as Theodosius the Great became the Roman Emperor in 375 C.E. The Christian Church triumphed under his reign as he put forth an edict for the destruction of Paganism.

Theophilus was the patriarch of Alexandria and in reality the ruler of this great city. He followed the edict of his Emperor in Rome by allowing violence to unfold here. He was a very passionate man with an utterly ruthless nature.

The two factions, Christian and Pagan, were already at each other's throats, and many people had been killed. Theophilus added fuel to the simmering fire by inciting the Christians to riot.

Soon a murderous mob ran through the streets of Alexandria. They smashed and destroyed anything that was Pagan. Many Pagans were killed by the Christian mob as they rioted. The great temple called the Serapeum contained incredible treasures. Gold and silver ornaments, marble statues, and other fine wealth filled this place. These suffered at the hands of the mob as this famous building was turned to ruin. This temple proper was only a part of the huge Alexandrian Library complex that sprawled out over a large area of Alexandria. This great library system consisted of the main or Great Library, the Museum, and the sister Library of the Serapeum that contained hallways and porticoes full of books and scrolls connected to the main temple itself. In essence, Alexandria was a city full of books and scrolls.

For over two hundred years, Christians had been persecuted by Pagan Rome. Now, a chance to repay the Pagans in kind had arrived. Blood for blood was the result. Hatred ran through the Christians like an epidemic.

Hypatia was the daughter of a famous mathematician and astronomer named Theon. She was beautiful, highly intelligent, and educated. As a philosopher and astronomer herself, Hypatia surpassed all others including the highly trained men who were associated with the Alexandrian Library and Museum.

She had studied in the ancient mystery schools of Egypt and was now one of their priests and teachers. Students came from all over the Roman world to study at her feet. She excelled in philosophy, astrology, astronomy, mathematics, mysticism, and ancient wisdoms. A kinder, gentler, and more loving person could not be found. The beauty of her soul matched the great beauty of her physical features.

Hypatia was nervous as she drove her chariot through the streets towards the Great Library. The two white horses that pulled her along seemed to share in her nervousness.

She had been advised by some of her learned friends to stay away from open areas and to remain indoors. This independent woman refused to be ruled by fear. She felt she was entitled to her Pagan beliefs. Although she appreciated the advice, her intention was to return to her study room at the Alexandrian Library. This was where she felt most at home, in the hallways and rooms of the huge library system.

Her mind focused on these thoughts as she shook the reins of her chariot and urged the horses to a faster pace. They sped down a wide street past several buildings. Up ahead the street opened up onto a large, open square. White stones covered the ground of this spacious area.

As Hypatia's chariot came out of the street and onto the stone covered square, she slowed her beautiful horses to a walk. She glanced about. Something felt wrong. The hair on the back of her neck stood up. Her heart started to beat faster. The yelling and screaming that Hypatia had heard in the distance as she had left her fine home now became very loud.

From everywhere men and women rushed towards her chariot. Angry people poured out of the Serapeum temple just to her right.

"Kill her, kill her!" screamed a short, dark-haired man as he grabbed at the leather bridles of the horses. He blocked Hypatia's chariot from moving ahead.

She looked behind her as she tried to draw the paired white team around and back toward the way she had come. It was to no avail. Her escape was closed off.

Christians full of bloodlust surrounded her chariot. A woman with curly hair snarled at Hypatia and threw a rock at her. The projectile hit her squarely in the left shoulder and bounced off. A terrible pain went through her whole left arm making it numb.

The assailant then pointed an accusing finger and yelled, "That's her! That's Hypatia, a leader of the Pagans!"

Terrified and confused, Alexandria's most famous female scholar cried, "Please, please let me go. I have done you no wrong."

Ignoring her pleas, many angry hands reached forward and dragged her from the car of her chariot. Hypatia's cries for mercy were lost amidst the shouts of the Christian mob.

They continued to drag her by her long hair and arms through the square and into a portico near the Serapeum temple itself. Sobs escaped Hypatia's lips as people began to kick and punch her. Some of the crowd spat on her and cursed her as a Pagan she-devil.

In moments the mob's helpless victim was covered in blood. The crimson color excited the rioters to a new level. Their bloodlust became uncontrollable as they literally pulled her apart; ripped her to pieces.

From that point, many of them started to run amok through the hallways, porticoes and rooms of part of the huge library complex. Books, scrolls, and precious documents were gathered and then thrown into a central area. Certain individuals brought torches to the rapidly mounting stockpile of written material and set it on fire.

Soon a bonfire burned amid the chaos and ruin. More papers, documents, and books were continually added to the growing fire.

Greek and Roman literature, ancient texts, sacred scriptures, and historical records were lost to the flames. Scrolls of papyrus containing knowledge of ancient Egypt and its forerunner Atlantis went up in smoke. The works of many philosophers, Roman emperors, scientists, and healers all met the same fate.

In that single event, thousands of books and scrolls containing invaluable knowledge were destroyed. Even poor Hypatia's own wonderful works were burnt.

The mob, in its hatred and rage, had caused a tremendous and irreplaceable loss to humanity. Intolerance for other peoples' beliefs had resulted in a terrible catastrophe. This was a blow that the world would never recover from.

The previous vision that the author received was told to you, the reader, for a special reason. It was presented to you in order to show the stupidity and uselessness of religious intolerance. The intent was not to make you angry but to open your eyes to the cruel nature that is inherent in us all. Pagans have persecuted Christians; Christians have persecuted Pagans. Muslims, Christians, and Jews today still hurt one another.

As you become more enlightened in our current society, many of you will strive to have an open and loving heart. The violent ways of the past will disappear as you embrace a more spiritual path.

A truly enlightened soul on earth embraces the truth and wisdom found in our many cultures and religions. All major religions, even with their individual and respective faults, still possess certain truths. For many of you, religion is a path, your path to the Creator, God, or Power. All of you must take a spiritual approach in your journey back to the Source or the Creator. For some of you, a spiritual path that does not involve an organized religion may be your way. For others, a particular religion, be it Wicca, Paganism, Christianity, Islam, Buddhism, or Hinduism, may be the road that you follow.

In any case, all lead back to the Creator if you develop a loving heart and treat others with respect and tolerance.

This brings to mind the following analogy. Six persons stood at the bottom of the mountain. Three were men and three were women. All were on their own spiritual journey back to God or the Creator. The top of the mountain that they stood before represented Spiritual Enlightenment and the Light of the Creator. Before each person was a dirt path that led up the mountain to the top. All six spiritual seekers started on their own separate paths heading upwards. Eventually, each one of then made it to the top of the mountain where both the Light and Spiritual Enlightenment existed. Even though each one followed his or her own path, they all finally made it back to the Source and attained true enlightenment.

This should be the goal for everyone.

> "Peace will come when each of us goes within, and realizes that we are all equal aspects of God; then we can all sit together in harmony . . ."
>
> —A Spiritual Warrior

Enjoy your spiritual journey!

Notes

Introduction

"Light shines out and joy pours forth . . ."
—Wise, Dead Sea Scrolls, column 27, 4Q, 427,
    fragment 7.

"That among the one hundred and twenty members . . ."
—Lewis, *The Secret Doctrines of Jesus,* 28.

"The first attack of the Sons of Light shall be undertaken against the forces of the Sons of Darkness, the army of Belial . . ."
—Wise, Dead Sea Scrolls, "The War Scroll," Column 1,
    1QM, 4Q, 491–496.

"In doubt if an action is just, abstain."
—Petras and Petras, *The Whole World Book of Quotations,* 3.
    Quotation by Zoroaster (c. 630–553 B.C.E.) in the Avesta.
    The Avesta is an ancient Iranian (Persian) religious text.
    For more on the Avesta, see bib. entry for Kapadia.

"Heaven is my father, the earth my mother . . ."
—Petras and Petras, *The Whole World Book of Quotations,*
    290. Quotation by Chang Tsai (1020–1077), Chinese
    philosopher, in "The Western Inscription."

Chapter One

"If there is anything lovely, if there is anything desirable . . ."
—Sri Ramatherin, *Unto Thee I Grant,* 4:59.

Chapter Two

"Look within. Within is the fountain of good . . ."
—Eliot, *The Meditations of Marcus Aurelius,* 251. Quota-
    tion by Marcus Aurelius, Roman emperor and philoso-
    pher (121–180 C.E.).

Chapter Three

"The mind of man is capable of anything . . ."
—Conrad, *Heart of Darkness.*

"No man is free who is not master of himself."
—Epictetus, *The Golden Sayings of Epictetus,* 184.

Chapter Four

"All that we are is the result of what we have thought . . ."
—Easwaran, *Dhammapada: Collections of Ancient Buddhist
    Poems and Aphorisms,* 79. Quotation by Dhammapada
    (c. third century B.C.E.).

"Wisdom makes her sons exalted . . ."
—Skehan, *The Wisdom of Ben Sira.* Quotation by Ben Sira
    (c. second century B.C.E.), Hebrew scholar and philoso-
    pher. Also found in: Petras and Petras, *The Whole World
    Book of Quotations,* 305.

"Riches are not from abundance of worldly goods, but from a contented mind. . . ."

—Usmani, The Noble Qu'ran. Quotation by Muhammad (570–632 C.E.), Prophet of Islam.

Chapter Five

"There is a light that shines beyond all things on earth . . ."

—Petras and Petras, *The Whole World Book of Quotations,* 266. Quotation by Chandogya Upanishad (c. seventh and eighth century B.C.E.) in the Upanishads, sacred philosophical Hindu literature.

"You can sense energy to the degree your heart is open and loving . . ."

—Roman, *Personal Power Through Awareness,* 18. Sanaya Roman is a New Age author.

Chapter Six

"The most beautiful experience we can have is the mystical. It is the power of true art and science."

—Frank, *Einstein: His Life and Times,* 12:5. Quote by Albert Einstein.

"Doing good to others in not a duty. It is joy, for it increases your own health and happiness."

—Kapadia, *Teachings of Zoroaster and the Philosophy of the Parsi Religion.* Quotation by Zoroaster. Also found in: Zubco, *Treasury of Spiritual Wisdom,* 200.

Chapter Seven

"Human energy is low and the Divine Energy is . . ."

—Svennson, *Chandogya Upanishad: With Comments from the Writings of Bhagavan Sri Sathya Sai Baba.* Quotation by Sathya Sai Baba.

"Nothing in life is to be feared, it is only to be understood."

—Petras and Petras, *The Whole World Book of Quotations,* 93. Quotation by Marie Curie (1867–1939), French scientist.

Chapter Eight

"Limited in his nature, infinite in his desires, man is a fallen god who remembers the heavens."

—Zubco, *Treasury of Spiritual Wisdom,* 126. Quoatation by Alphonse de Lamartine (1790–1869) in *Meditations Poetiques.*

"Earth has no sorrow that Heaven can not heal."

—Zubco, *Treasury of Spiritual Wisdom,* 242. Quotation by Thomas Moore in the song "Come, Ye Disconsolate."

Chapter Nine

"Man, tree, and flower are supposed to die . . ."

—Zubco, *Treasury of Spiritual Wisdom,* 270. Quotation by Mary Baker Eddy in *Inspirations for Life's Relationships: Quotations from Mary Baker Eddy.*

Chapter Ten

"There is only one good—knowledge, and one evil—ignorance."

—Zubco, *Treasury of Spiritual Wisdom,* 200. Quotation by Socrates in Xenophon's *Conversations of Socrates.*

"Peace will come when each of us goes within . . ."

—Zubco, *Treasury of Spiritual Wisdom,* 354. Quotation by a Spiritual Warrior.

Bibliography

Conrad, Joseph. *Heart of Darkness*. Boston: Charles E. Tuttle, 1997.

Davis, A. Powell. *The Meaning of the Dead Sea Scrolls*. New York: The New American Library (Mentor Books), 1956.

De Lamartine, Alphonse. *Meditations Poetiques*. Lewiston, NY: Edwin Mellen Press, 1993.

De Long, Douglas. *Ancient Teachings for Beginners*. St. Paul, MN: Llewellyn Publications, 2000.

Easwaran, Eknath. *The Dhammapada: Collections of Ancient Buddhist Poems and Aphorisms*. Tomales, CA: Nilgiri Press, 1986.

Eddy, Mary Baker. *Inspiration for Life's Relationships: Quotations from Mary Eddy Baker*. Boston: Christian Science (The Writings of Mary Eddy Baker), 2003.

Eliot, Charles W., ed. *The Meditations of Marcus Aurelius*. Danbury, CT: The Harvard Classics, Grolier Enterprises, 1980.

Epictetus. *The Golden Sayings of Epictetus*. Danbury, CT: The Harvard Classics, Grolier Enterprises, 1980.

Frank, Phillip. *Einstein: His Life and Times*. George Rosen, trans. New York: DaCapo Press, 2002.

Kapadia, S. A. *Teachings of Zoroaster and the Philosophy of the Parsi Religion*. Whitefish, MT: Kessinger Publishing, 1998.

Lewis, H. Spencer. *The Secret Doctrines of Jesus*. Los Angeles, CA: AMORC, 1987.

Merriam-Webster, ed. *Webster's New Explorer Dictionary of Quotations*. Springfield, MA: Merriam-Webster Incorporated, 2000.

Parsons, Edward Alexander. *The Alexandrian Library: Glory of the Hellenic World*. New York: The Elsevier Press, 1952.

Petras, Kathryn, and Ross Petras. *The Whole World Book of Quotations: Wisdom from Women and Men Around the Globe Throughout the Centuries*. New York: Addison-Wesley, 1995.

Roman, Sanaya. *Personal Power Through Awareness*. Tiburon, CA: H. J. Kramer, 1986.

Seymour, Tryntje Van Ness. *The Gift of Changing Woman*. New York: Henry Holt and Company, 1993.

Skehan, Patrick. *The Wisdom of Ben Sira*. New York: Doubleday & Company, 1990.

Sri Ramatherin, ed. *Unto Thee I Grant*. 32nd edition, vol. 5. San Jose, CA: AMORC, 1979.

Svennson, Camille, ed. *Chandogya Upanishad: With Comments from the Writings of Bhagavan Sri Sathya Sai Baba*. Tustin, CA: Sathya Sai Baba Book Center of America, 2000.

Tortoro, Gerald J. *Principles of Anatomy and Physiology*. 7th edition, New York: Harper Collins, 1993.

Usmani, Allama Shabbir Ahmad. *The Noble Qu'ran: Tafseer-e-usman*, 3 vols. North Haledon, NJ: Islamic Publications International, 1999.

Wise, Michael, et al. *The Dead Sea Scrolls: A New Translation*. San Francisco, CA: Harper Collins Publishers, 1996.

Xenophon, et al. *Conversations of Socrates*. New York: Penguin Classics, 1990.

Zubco, Andy. *Treasury of Spiritual Wisdom*. San Diego, CA: Blue Dove Press, 1996.

About the Author

Douglas De Long (Canada) is an energy healer and medical intuitive. He works as a past-life therapist, chakra master, counselor, and spiritual teacher. In the past twelve years, he has regressed 800 people and taught psychic development to several hundred clients and students.